The Fifteen-Second Secret

The Fifteen-Second Secret

LARRY JONES

THOMAS NELSON PUBLISHERS
Nashville

Published in Nashville, Tennessee, by Thomas Nelson,
Inc., and distributed in Canada by Lawson Falle, Ltd.,
Cambridge, Ontario.

Scripture quotations are from the NEW KING JAMES
VERSION of the Bible, copyright © 1983, 1982, 1980,
1979, by Thomas Nelson Publishers.

Library of Congress Cataloging-in-Publication Data

Jones, Larry.
    The fifteen-second secret / Larry Jones.
        p.   cm.
    ISBN 0-8407-3340-2
    1. Christian life—1960– I. Title. II. Title:
15-second secret.
BV4501.2.J654   1991
248.4—dc20   91-3317
                                                     CIP

Printed in the United States of America

1 2 3 4 5 6 7 — 95 94 93 92 91 90

Dedicated
to
Frances Jones,
my wife,
who has always
known the secret.

Contents

Preface

People make life too difficult.

The truly profound teachers have always stated their
insights simply and to the point. The story I am about to
tell you is of that order. My story arises out of my own
discovery of how the most significant clues to successful
living come in small, easily understood portions. While
it's hard to do what we know we should, the path we can
take is clearly marked.

The principle holds true for the secret serenity of life.
You can find the answer if you take small enough bites of
the problem and digest each one before going on. I want
to help you discover how to break the problem down into
manageable parts.

After the Vietnam War, one of the most poignant descriptions of the ordeal of prisoners of war was Colonel
Robinson Risner's *The Passing of the Night*. The senior
banking officer in the notorious Hanoi Hilton, Colonel
Risner offers a moving and telling account of his faith
and trials during his imprisonment.

One of the beliefs that helped him through his seven-
and-a-half-year nightmare was that he could take any

amount of punishment or temptation for sixty seconds. As I read, I thought of the relevance to everyday life. We must not live in days or weeks, months or years, but moment by moment, sixty seconds at a time.

In 1982 I read another book that applied the time concept to the realm of business: *The One-Minute Manager*, a stunning best-seller. In a simple and straightforward way, the authors described how to base good business management practices on principles that could be practiced in one minute.

Now I am going to share with you the ultimate use of time. In only *fifteen seconds* you can change your life and find new power for living each day. Want to find serenity? It'll only take a second.

Larry Jones

The Fifteen-Second Secret

ONE _____

The
Quest

Once a troubled but sincere young woman was seeking the secret of well-being.

To her deep consternation, Hope Moore could not remember ever having met a person who lived a normal everyday life and also enjoyed genuine peace of mind. She had popular friends, affluent business associates, competent clients, well educated peers, disciplined jogging partners, and highly determined children. But none of her associates felt inner calm.

When Hope Moore had been married thirteen years, she realized that the sparkle had gone out of her marriage. A year later she and her husband found themselves living in the same house but as distant from each other as wounded strangers could get. The emotional void increased her inner longing for a stable and substantive basis for her life. She grabbed at every novelty that surfaced. When the New Wave books and tapes began circulating, Hope eagerly devoured them. Whenever a fad marched by, Hope lined up to join the parade.

Being a persistent person and having exhausted all of the quick-fix cures, Saturday sedative seminars, and the pop how-to-books, she desperately began to seek serenity.

Her first stop was with the psychology industry. On a friend's recommendation, she found a counselor to help her explore the source of her problem. Quickly she was informed that the heart of her dilemma was a poorly developed sense of identity. If she could unravel the mystery of who she was, well-being would surely follow.

The sessions were doubled each week so that Hope could get in at least two to three hours of counseling a week. Between sessions the seeker devoured the latest in self-fulfillment and insight-producing books. She was making considerable improvement until the first month's billing arrived. Struggling with depression over the bill, Hope suffered a significant setback.

Nevertheless, she was undaunted. Mortgaging her house, she continued therapy nonstop for a year-and-a-half. During those weeks, the therapist unraveled Hope's psyche the way a cook peels away the layers of an onion. Finally her life was laid out with all the observable pieces in order. One morning she sat down to consider what her emotional explorations meant.

Unfortunately, as she looked at all the pieces, she saw only fragmentation. Surely an onion was more than the sum of its layers! At least the seeker hoped she was. But all the disjointed segments of her past provided her no sense of continuity, connectedness, and cohesion. Clearly she hadn't found peace!

The sincere young woman had just taken a year-and-a-half detour. Shocked by her discovery and hoping to avoid repeating her mistake, Hope Moore sought a new path. Since community service and philanthropic activities had been good for others, they should work for her. Perhaps a hitch with Big Sisters or the bell ringers at Christmas would help.

Sure enough! Hope Moore took great satisfaction from helping others. Sensing that she was on to something, the seeker began filling every spare moment with altruistic pursuits.

Monday became YWCA council day when she dispensed management advice. Tuesday was Brownies afternoon with little girls. Wednesday became arts and humanities morning with committees that worked on community projects. Thursday was to be left open, but a chance to join the local zoo board arose, and she did enjoy animals. Friday was the time to help a local political committee to elect the right candidates. Those responsibilities spilled over into Saturday and ended up taking time on Sunday afternoon. Hope found that she had to run hard to get to all the places where she might find peace of mind. Not once did she reflect on the fact that she was actually spending no time at all trying to mend her relationship with her husband.

Hope didn't have much time left to reflect on what she was doing until she became ill. A routine cold turned into pneumonia that appeared to be chronic. She was *really* sick.

"Sorry," the doctor told her, "but your system is totally exhausted. You're not recovering because the pace you keep has destroyed your resistance."

"I've only been trying to find peace of mind," Hope explained. "I exercise every day." Hope was an attractive woman with dark brown hair. She always kept her appearance in tip-top condition. But she realized her face did look rather gaunt. "I am thin, maybe a little too thin," she admitted.

"Well, you can't take any more," the physician warned, "or you're going to be dead. So go easy on all the calm you've been trying to accumulate, or we'll be holding your funeral."

Looking out the window of her hospital room, Hope knew that she had completely missed her goal. If she increased her activity to find serenity, she would be history before she even came close. She had failed again.

There must be an easier, quicker way.

In front of her was a newspaper with an ad for a self-improvement course. No question about it! The company promised quick, effective, and total results to those who invested a mere twelve weeks and $2,500. Hope could improve her memory, approach relationships more confidently, relax in front of groups, and develop total confidence. In addition, bonus New Wave lessons would reveal techniques of extrasensory perception and the use of the unconscious mind.

"Why didn't I try this school in the first place?" Hope asked aloud. "Obviously these people cost less and produce more. I'll sign up immediately—well . . . as soon as I'm well enough."

Months later, on the day of her graduation, the instructor handed Hope a diploma certifying that she was now a genuine *"world beater."* Assertively she took the paper from his hands, bowed to the applauding audience, and marched off the stage. "I can, I can, I can," she muttered defiantly to herself—as she had been taught. "If I can believe it, I can do it!" Her new mottoes were her key to the future.

The New Wave component of her program had promised to teach Hope astral projection, travel right out of
her body. Lying on her bedroom floor, she tried the out-
of-body travels a number of times. She felt the exhilarat-
ing thrill of flying through space to far-off places where
she had always wanted to be a tourist.

One evening as Hope was flying "out of her body," she
heard the strange sound of a mystical presence passing in
front of her. She wondered if it was a reincarnated spirit.

"Need my slippers," a very familiar voice hummed.
"Don't worry, I'll step over you," her husband said. "Isn't
all this a little silly?"

Opening one eye, Hope saw him walk into the closet.
She did feel ridiculous. All her trips had been in her
head. But she shut her eyes so he wouldn't know.

For three weeks Hope stood in front of the mirror every
morning. She went through her enthusiasm routine, flex-
ing her motivational muscles. Pumped full of emotional
adrenaline, she hit the streets feeling higher than a kite.
Somewhere in the fourth week, a disconcerting thought
crossed her mind: Hype is not the same as health.

As the platitudes began dissolving in her mind, the
seeker had a terrible *deja vu* sensation. She knew what
was coming next. At least this time recognition only took
weeks and not years. But the disappointment seemed
much deeper and darker. Once more serenity had proven
completely elusive.

At that moment the sincere young woman realized
what she had missed in her search: Her quest *for* serenity
was actually a flight *from* fear. Her inner descent into her
own mind and emotions was prompted by her hope to
escape something that she couldn't even name yet. The
frantic activity of her many clubs and organizations was
an attempt to run fast enough to escape an unseen spec-

ter. Yet all of the enthusiasm and exercises in the world couldn't erase what seemed to be lurking behind her boundlessly energetic approach. Hope had tried to become a "world beater" because of her fear that the world would beat her!

She was really discouraged.

"What can I do?" she asked her best friend. "I'm really at the end of my rope. I don't know what's left."

"Strange," her friend said, "but recently I had an amazing experience. I think that for the first time I met a truly "altogether" person. I've seen this man many times, but the other day we talked for the first time. He was the most insightful, thoughtful person I've ever talked with. He was loaded with common sense and caring. I believe I've found the person for you."

"Really?" Hope Moore's eyes widened. "Where?"

"You probably aren't going to believe this—" Her friend shook her head. "But he's my mail carrier."

"You're joking," the seeker laughed.

"No." Her friend shook her head again. "I asked about him, and many people said that where this postman goes, he leaves joy with the mail. I noticed that he always left me feeling tranquil. So I began talking with him. He is truly a peaceful man."

"How interesting!"

"As we talked, he made me feel important. He looked into my eyes so honestly that I knew he was for real."

"Could I meet him?"

"I have no doubt that if you called him, he would be glad to talk with you."

"A postman?" Hope was thinking about all of the psychologists, counselors, and professional people-fixers she had met over the years. "Well, I've tried everything else.

Maybe he knows how to bring me some good news for a change."

"I think so," her friend encouraged her. "Here's his phone number."

Hope reached the postman that evening and told him why she was calling. She asked if he would be willing to talk with her. He responded graciously and invited her to come any evening. Perhaps she would be wasting her time, but then the record of how she had spent her time during the last several years wasn't anything to brag about. Hope made an appointment.

Hanging up the phone, she cocked her head, pursed her lips, and sighed, "Here's hoping. . . ."

Three days later, Hope drove up in front of the postman's house. All of her other attempts had failed, so her confidence was low. She had lost her ability to expect much. Timidly she knocked on the door.

"You're the woman who called." The older man was almost charming in his warmth and openness.

"I'm sorry to bother you," she apologized, "but I do hope to have a word with you."

"Of course," he smiled. His gray hair and blue eyes seemed especially piercing, and yet his countenance was kind. "My name is Sterling Veteran."

"I'm Hope Moore." She offered her hand. "I am told that you know the secret of serenity, Mr. Veteran."

"Come in. I'd be pleased to talk with you." When the seeker came in, he followed her down the hall.

"I'm always glad when someone asks about the most important lesson I've learned." He pointed toward a chair. "Do sit down."

"You're a postman?" Immediately Hope realized that her tone sounded a little too condescending.

"You've never met a happy letter carrier?" he laughed. "The truth is that happiness doesn't have a thing in the world to do with where you work. Lots of folks keep changing positions hoping to find the golden ring with the right job."

"Of course." Hope looked pensive as she remembered all the approaches she had tried in the last three years. "That's a temptation," she groaned.

"People look for peace of mind in the strangest places." Mr. Veteran folded his arms. "I observe all the options on my daily rounds. Mail carriers go everywhere, you know."

"Well, wherever you go," the young seeker said enthusiastically, "people are impressed. My friend says that you're the most serene man in this community, Mr. Veteran."

"Just call me Sterling." He nodded, then shook his head. "I wasn't always so composed. For a good hunk of my life I was a nervous wreck most of the time. Everything felt completely out of control."

"You sure don't look as if you were ever frenzied."

"Oh, but I was!" He ran his hands through his graying hair. "Until I learned the fifteen-second secret I was a mess. The secret made all the difference!"

"Fifteen seconds?" the young seeker exclaimed. "I've spent years trying to find out the ingredients in tranquility. Fifteen seconds?"

"When you know what you're doing," Sterling grinned, "it doesn't take long."

"I've talked with many people," Hope explained rapidly, "and done a lot of things trying to find just some of the joy you seem to have so much of. Could you share your secret with me?"

"I must warn you—" Sterling leaned forward looking straight into her eyes "—if you use this secret you will never be the same again. Are you prepared to make a change that will affect every area of your life?"

"I've come here," Hope pleaded, "because I've tried everything else and nothing has worked. I am definitely ready."

"Well," he said, "the secret's not hard and the idea's not too complex to put into practice." He turned his head skeptically, "But most people want something difficult and bizarre. My secret is just as obvious as your own nose. That's probably why you've been missing it."

"Yes?" The seeker beckoned for Mr. Veteran to continue. "Don't stop now."

The postman leaned back in his chair. "People like to tell a good story, but the secret isn't just something to kick around in your head." He began rocking. "Got to practice it or it won't work at all."

"Hum . . ." Hope scratched her head. "I don't understand."

"Can't prove some things by believing them," he instructed. "You know that they're true only after you have practiced what they teach you."

"Definitely." The young seeker had no idea what she was agreeing to, but the wait was taking its toll. "I'm ready right now to go to work."

"Work, you say?" Sterling sat up in his chair. "Nope, that's a problem too. Everybody makes everything too hard. They try to do it all by themselves. Yes, that's the paradox."

"But I can do anything I put my mind to," Hope Moore protested.

"No, you can't." Sterling smiled, but his voice was

firm. "Life is filled with things you can't accomplish no matter how hard you try. The longer you live, the more you will discover impossibilities. For example, you're frustrated because you *can't* manufacture peace. It's a gift."

The seeker blinked. "A gift?" she asked slowly. "How did you discover such a thing?"

"From an ancient book," Sterling answered. "In fact, it was written about twenty-five hundred years ago."

"Wow!" the young seeker gasped. "Hidden knowledge from a lost civilization."

"Not lost . . ." the postman explained, "just neglected."

"What did the book say?"

"I've memorized the words," Sterling said, closing his eyes and settling back in his chair, "so that I can call them to mind in fifteen seconds or less." Slowly he recited, "The happy man 'will not be afraid of evil tidings; his heart is steadfast, trusting in the LORD'" (Ps. 112:7).

"I don't understand." Hope shook her head. "Why do those words give you peace?"

"Let me put the ideas into my own words. Happy people aren't afraid of bad news because they have their emotions tied down. They know that God has everything under control."

"Okay," Hope said, folding her arms, "I understand what you just said, but I'm not sure how it could possibly fit me. My emotions go wild when I hear threatening information."

"Of course." Sterling's voice was sympathetic. "Most people tend to let their emotions run them, and that's why they're unhappy. They don't stand on firm ground."

"You show me where to put my feet," Hope answered,

"and I'm with you. I'd love to know how to keep from being swamped with fear."

"The secret works like this. . . ." Sterling opened his eyes again. "When you are faced with bad news, a difficult situation, or a devastating diagnosis, you make an important decision immediately. In the first fifteen seconds you decide what you are going to do with the facts. As a mailman I watch people receive staggering information every day. In a fourth of a minute they will determine their emotional response to everything that follows."

"Fifteen seconds?" Hope looked skeptical.

"Watch people open their mail," Sterling continued. "As you follow their eyes, you'll immediately see their reactions written all over their faces. As soon as they come to the punch line, they either smile, frown, gasp, or, often, cry. Their responses are formed in a split second."

"And what are you suggesting is happening to them?"

"They immediately decide whether they will face the future with *faith* or *fear*. One of those perspectives will dominate their responses."

"Oh, my goodness." Hope put her hand to her mouth. "I've never thought of it that way before. I'm always afraid of what's going to happen next—even before I know all the facts—particularly when I hear bad news."

"What you feel-think-do is predicated on your perception of the facts." Sterling winked and continued, "That's why you can never have peace of mind. When you build on fear, the foundation's always shaky, isn't it?"

Hope Moore nodded her head in stunned agreement.

"Now, the other way," the mailman lectured, "is to build on trust so that everything you hope for rests on faith. Serenity begins in your personal certainty."

"How do you know this approach is true?" The young woman scratched her head. "What basis do I have for choosing faith over fear?"

"The people who wrote the ancient book proved it!" Sterling answered. "The entire history of their civilization certifies their discovery that the one true God was always going before them preparing the path that they had to travel. They knew that he had an answer for their bad news before they had even received it. Amazing?"

"Amazing!" She nodded. "How did you discover this idea?"

"If you really want to know, you'll have to hear about my grandfather." Sterling settled back in his chair.

"Sure," Hope smiled. "I love grandfather stories."

"You would have liked my grandfather," Sterling beamed. "He was the wisest man I ever knew. Had an uncanny sense of things. Just loaded with common sense."

"He taught you about the Bible?"

"Sure did. We lived out on the farm where he and my grandmother had a house next to ours. Spent lots of time together, even went to church together on Sunday. When we came home, he explained what I'd heard. Remember the story of Moses?"

"Oh, yes," Hope smiled. "I've heard of him."

"Grandpa particularly liked this story. I can remember his vivid accounts of how Moses led the people of Israel through the wilderness. He described the great pillar of fire guiding the children of Israel at night and the amazing cloud going before them in the day. Those amazing sights swirled around in my imagination."

"But how did his stories help you develop your faith?"

"My grandfather pointed out that Moses always knew that God was going before him. Just as the fire and the cloud gave the people the right directions, so God was way ahead of any need or problem that might arise. Before the people of Israel even became afraid, God was providing them with answers. Anticipating that they could get lost, God provided direction. He established light before the darkness came. Get the point?"

"What an extraordinary insight." Hope rubbed her chin. "Your grandfather was quite a thinker."

"Far more than a philosopher," the mailman replied, "he was a man of faith who truly believed that God had the answers before we had the problems."

"I wish I could be that sort of a person," Hope sighed.

"You can be," Sterling said firmly, "if you learn the meaning of four key words—and the first one is omniscience. That big word means that God is all-knowing. My grandfather understood the practical implications of believing that God already has everything figured out."

"But how can that be?" Hope pursed her lips. "Surely lots of my problems are purely the result of chance—of fate."

"Now that's where you get in trouble," Sterling warned. "When you start basing your confidence on playing the odds, you end up with a slot-machine mentality. Your security depends on pulling the right levers and hoping the spinning wheels stop in your favor. To be happy you have to base your confidence in something that can stand the test of time."

"Like what?"

"Well . . ." Sterling reached for a black book. "Let's read from the book that I was speaking about a few moments ago. These pages tell the stories of people whose lives demonstrate God's omniscience. Here's the most important story of all. Listen to this: 'He indeed was foreordained before the foundation of the world, but was manifest in these last times for you' (1 Pet. 1:20)."

Sterling leaned back in his chair, rubbed his chin, and thought for a moment before he explained "God had a plan for us even before there was a world. Nothing that happens is beyond his control. While bad things do happen to us, he still is at work to turn them into benefits. Even if you can't understand it, he is at work on your behalf right now."

"I've never heard of such a suggestion," Hope answered. "God planned events, things, people, before the world—even before time began."

"Right!" Sterling grinned and said, "Sort of blows your mind, doesn't it? Now look at another story that describes how God took care of Moses."

"All right. I'm all ears."

"Notice these words," Sterling's finger followed the line, "that tell you how God was helping Moses. He led him, 'to bring you into the place which I have prepared for you' (Ex. 23:20). God had picked out a homeland for Moses before he was even born. Moses didn't know what place, but God had already deeded it to him."

"You've really covered a lot of ground."

"Omniscience is a big word! And we're talking about a big God." Sterling started thumbing through the pages again. "That's why faith can be stronger than fear. God knew what was best for you before your birth."

Hope threw up her hands. "Why didn't someone tell me about these ideas sooner?"

"But I'm not through yet," Sterling continued. "God's knowledge also extends into the future. He's already on top of what is yet to be. Tell me, what is your greatest fear?"

"I guess . . ." Hope paused and thought carefully.

"Everyone is afraid of dying. I think death is the hardest problem to face."

"Well, listen to this section then." Sterling stopped at another place. "Jesus of Nazareth is talking about death in these lines. 'In My Father's house are many mansions; if it were not so, I would have told you. I go to prepare a place for you. And if I go and prepare a place for you, I will come again and receive you to Myself' (John 14:2–3). He takes care of death before we get to it. Your worst fear has already been covered."

"I am simply astonished." The young seeker rocked back in her chair. "Amazed!"

"Now my young friend," Sterling said, tapping the Bible, "if God has taken care of everything from the beginning of time to the end, why should you worry about the in-between? Omniscience allows you to depend on the Creator, not chance."

"What a relief that would be," Hope confessed. "My life has always been centered on problems. No matter where I turn, I seem to get mired down in my dilemmas as if I keep stepping into a swamp. On the other hand," she smiled, "your focus is entirely on the solution."

"That's the big difference." Sterling shook his finger. "I don't let the problem get a grip on me."

She pursed her lips and said, "I'm not sure that I could ever do that. When things go wrong, I'm afraid, the difficulties just get under my skin."

"Grandpa called that negative faith," Sterling acknowledged. "You're believing—but in the wrong thing."

"Negative faith?"

"Sure. Most people spend all their time meditating on potential disaster instead of on promised assistance. Let me show you something."

Sterling thumbed through the back section of his

Bible. "As a child I heard the minister preach on this portion, but I didn't get it. After Grandpa explained, I understood what positive faith was."

"Please read it to me," Hope asked.

"I will," Sterling affirmed. "But first let's look at the reason we just naturally seem to start with negative faith. Have you ever wondered why fear is so easy and faith so difficult?"

"I've never thought of it that way before," Hope answered, "but you are absolutely right. What should be the best response seems to be too hard."

"When Peter described the futile ways inherited from our fathers, he was talking about a universal problem. Even though God's way is obviously best for us, we don't really want what he wants. Each of us would prefer to live life according to our set of rules. As in the song, we'd rather do it 'my way.' The name for that tendency is sin. Sin isn't something we do; it's the way we are. The tendency infects our ideas, decisions, dreams, and hopes. We inherently know that because we have not followed his way, we have something to be worried about. So we end up captured by fear. Sin is our number one human problem."

"Sin is at the root of our negative fear?" Hope frowned, unsure of what Sterling meant.

"Exactly!"

"But I always thought that sins are the little naughty things people do. Some sins are bigger than others, but people have varying opinions about their seriousness."

"Sin and sins are two different matters," Sterling pointed out. "Sin is a condition. Like an infection in your body, sin is an invasion in your thoughts. It is a crack in the foundation. Sure, people have trivialized sins as if they were quaint little no-no's. But sin is a fatal disease that we all struggle with to the day we die."

"My goodness!" Hope gasped. "We're talking serious business here."

"You bet," Sterling agreed. "That's why the life, death, and resurrection of Jesus are so important. Let's look at the complete passage that I referred to earlier. Peter wrote:

> knowing that you were not redeemed with corruptible things, like silver or gold, from your aimless conduct received by tradition from your fathers, but with the precious blood of Christ, as of a lamb without blemish and without spot. He indeed was foreordained before the foundation of the world, but was manifest in these last times for you who through Him believe in God, who raised Him from the dead and gave Him glory, that your faith and hope are in God.
>
> (1 Pet. 1:18–21)

"Peter wanted us to know that before we even sinned, Jesus was prepared as the answer to our impossible dilemma. How's that for having the answer before we knew that we had the problem?"

"So—our biggest problem was solved by God before he had even created the universe!" Hope could only nod her head. "Now *that* is positive faith!"

"Absolutely. I focus on God's answer, not my problem."

"Amazing!"

"So," Sterling said, "the secret of serenity is that regardless of what happens, I immediately remember that I trust God's provision. I begin at this point."

"Two paths," the seeker mused, "and they do cross in my mind one hundred times every day."

"To paraphrase Robert Frost, I take the least traveled path," Mr. Veteran pointed out, "and that makes all the difference."

"Faith or fear," she said, more to herself than to him.

"The secret of serenity is a fifteen-second decision for faith." Sterling squeezed Hope's hand.

Later that evening Hope sat at her living room table, reflecting on her conversation with Sterling Veteran. "I believe my talks with the mailman are going to be very important," she said aloud. "I'm going to keep a notebook on what we talk about because I don't want to forget anything that might make the same difference in my life that I see in his."

She picked up a loose-leaf notebook that had been on the shelf for some time. Sure enough, at the back were a number of blank pages. Hope picked up a pencil and began to write.

Here's what she wrote on the first page:

1. *Remember:* In facing any difficulty, I will, in fifteen seconds, make a decision to face the issues either with faith or fear.

2. I have control over this decision, and the choice will make the difference between peace and confusion.

3. Sin is the number one human problem. Fear arises from my decision to put what I want ahead of what God intends.

4. The key is to remember that the Creator of the universe had an answer to my sin problem before the world ever came into being. The same is true of every problem I will ever know.

5. Faith is believing that God has already gone on before, bringing light and giving direction.

6. *Remember: omniscience.* God already knows everything there is to know about my problems and needs.

TWO

Fifteen-Second Convictions

Sterling Veteran left the room to get a cup of coffee. The young seeker, back for another visit, sat silently thinking about what she had been hearing. Hope struggled to know how to ask the right questions.

"I'm afraid your secret sounds too easy," she said hesitantly when the postman returned.

"Of course." He handed her a cup. "If I had told you something hard to believe, you'd have been ready to try it immediately. We all make life too difficult. You're reluctant because it doesn't seem to require enough of you."

"Well," the young seeker said, biting her lip, "I'm afraid you're right."

"Most of the really important commitments in life are

easy to talk about," Sterling explained, "but hard to do. Loving, caring, being disciplined—these are easy to describe but tough to do."

"But there must be more to the secret of serenity."

"I think you're doubting me," Sterling chuckled. "Perhaps you ought to visit with some of the people on my mail route. They might be able to help you resolve your reservations."

"Maybe some others *could* help give me a broader perspective." Hope tried to not sound as dubious as she felt.

"Sure." Sterling reached for a list on the top of his desk. "I have two names right here. They will understand and be sympathetic. Just drop by and tell either of them you're trying to figure out how the fifteen-second secret works."

"Okay," Hope agreed, "I'll go see them."

"You're going to be learning about the meaning of four very important concepts. After you discover how they apply to your life, you will be able to live by faith."

"Four concepts?" Hope asked, puzzled. "You only told me about one word."

"Let me give you all four. As you talk to my friends, you'll actually be exploring the definitions of these very important ideas. The four words are omnipotence, omniscience, omnipresence, and omnicaring."

"We've got a good start with omniscience."

"Got some real surprises ahead for you," Sterling laughed. "Good luck."

Hope Moore thanked the mailman for his kindness and the addresses. While she had some reservations, she also knew that if the task had been truly difficult, she would have tried it without any second thoughts. So with the addresses in one hand and her keys in the other, the seeker set out to find out what it might mean to decide automatically to live by faith and not fear.

The first address Sterling had given her wasn't that far away. The seeker read slowly, "Carol Singer, 2324 Calm Street." Since the home was only six blocks away, Hope called to see if it was convenient for her to drop by. Carol told her to come at once. Immediately, Hope drove to the attractive brown house, and she was warmly welcomed in to chat.

Carol Singer was an attractive middle-aged homemaker who quickly made the young seeker feel at home as they sat at her kitchen table. With an impish smile Carol asked, "So you've been to see my postman?"

"That's right," Hope replied. "I'm not sure what to think about him."

"I call him the holder of the fifteen-second secret," Carol laughed. "Most efficient man alive."

"Fifteen-second secret?"

"Yep," Carol explained, "that's really what makes him tick. He's learned the art of putting his important decisions into fifteen-second segments. Did he tell you about his fifteen-second secret?"

"He did. I've never heard anything like that in my life. I thought at first he was kidding. But he really isn't, is he?"

Mrs. Singer laughed. "He has a great sense of humor, but if there's one thing he doesn't joke about, it's the fifteen-second process."

The young seeker shrugged her shoulders and said, "I guess it all sounds too easy." She paused and added, "But then I'm not sure that I understand what it means to live by faith."

"Oh, I can tell you about that piece of the puzzle,"

Carol answered. "My fifteen-second convictions have made the secret truly work for me."

"Fifteen-second convictions!" Hope threw up her hands. "Here we go again. What in the world are fifteen-second convictions?"

"The truth of the matter is," Carol said slowly and carefully, "life is filled with a lot of hard knocks. No matter how good a person Sterling Veteran is, he does have to deliver lots of heartbreaking news. We have to know how to sort out the depressing experiences."

"Sure," the young seeker agreed. "I've had a few bad breaks."

"Fifteen-second convictions help us face the bad news."

"Give me an example," the sincere young woman asked.

"Okay," Carol nodded. "Every Sunday afternoon, I set aside time to address my major concern or problem, or sometimes it's a very special opportunity. I take pencil and paper and I write, 'My major concern for this next week is . . .' Then I write out clearly the issues I must face. After I'm clear about those problems, I follow with this statement: 'I believe God . . .' and I write in one hundred words or less what I believe about God in relation to my situation. If I have more than one major concern, I follow the same procedure with it. Most times, though, I only write about one difficulty. Those convictions guide me the rest of the week."

Hope Moore's face showed both comprehension and puzzlement. "Can you be more specific?" she asked.

"Well," Carol said, slowly rubbing her forehead, "I suppose that I might tell you about facing the worst news of my life. Living through it seemed completely impossible at the time."

The seeker leaned back in her chair and folded her arms.

"My next-door neighbor was the first to burst in with the news." Mrs. Singer looked out the window for a moment. "And then the policemen came. Actually it took a while to piece the whole story together."

Hope could feel the tension building and realized she might be about to hear more than she had bargained for.

"Our tragedy happened four years ago," Carol continued, "when my little girl, Linda, was riding her bicycle home from the park. A drunk driver jumped a curb and hit her on the sidewalk. She was killed instantly."

"Oh, no!" Hope gasped. "How horrible! I can't even imagine the pain that must have consumed you. How could you stand such a thing? Did your faith in God sustain you?"

"Well, actually, no. In fact, I blamed God for letting my daughter be killed. And if it hadn't been for Sterling, I might still be doing that."

The young woman's eyes widened. "What did he have to do with your not blaming God?"

"He'd been on this route for fifteen or twenty years and read about Linda's accident in the newspaper. A few days later . . ." Carol stopped and reached for a small picture of her daughter and handed it to Hope.

"On a Sunday afternoon, about a week 'after the accident, there was a knock at the door. Sterling had come with his wife, Joy, whom I had never met."

"When I invited them in, he didn't waste any time explaining why he had come. He just said, 'Mrs. Singer, we lost our son in Vietnam when he was just nineteen. He was our only child. We know how painful it is to lose a child. We also know how important our faith in God was in helping us through that time. From all the religious magazines that I've put in your mailbox through the years, I know you believe. But I wonder, is your faith helping you?'"

Carol Singer almost laughed. "Can you believe I exploded?" Then she bit her lip. "I was totally filled with anger that my little eleven-year-old girl would be killed by a drunk who was out on parole."

"How did Sterling respond?" the young woman asked. "I would have been terrified to face your wrath."

"Sterling wasn't. He said, 'Mrs. Singer, let's go to the dining room table.' There he pulled out some notebook paper and began writing. Then he showed me. 'Mrs. Singer's eleven-year-old daughter was run over and killed by a drunk driver last week. She can't help but blame God for it.'

"Holding the paper in front of me, he asked, 'Is that right Mrs. Singer?' I said, 'I'm afraid so.'

"Then he took the paper back and started writing again. When he showed it to me once more, he had written only three words: 'I believe God . . .' Then on another sheet, he wrote, 'God wants me to . . .' He stood up and said, 'Mrs. Singer, there's nothing more important for you as you go through this tragedy than knowing that God knows what you're experiencing. He loves you, and he is going before you. One way we can discover what is happening is to write down what we believe about God in relation to our loss and what he wants us to do about it. This process changed our lives.'"

"What did you do?" Hope asked. "I would think you would still be angry."

Carol thought for a few moments before answering. "Perhaps I was mostly hurt. Of course, I was also very confused. Actually I asked the postman why he thought any of this procedure would be of help to me."

"What did he say?"

"Sterling taught me a word that I didn't know before—omnipresence. New to you?"

"That's the second concept," Hope answered, "that he said I would need to learn. Tell me more."

"Sterling asked for my Bible and read me one of the promises. I have it memorized now: 'I will not leave you orphans; I will come to you' (John 14:18). He told me that omnipresence means that nothing can separate us from the presence of God. I may think that some condition of my life lies beyond the boundaries of God's care, but that's not true. He is always with me in every circumstance and situation."

"Then I bet he told you a story about his grandfather." Hope laughed.

"Sure did. Sterling's grandfather's parents were killed at the end of the last century when he was a small child. He ended up in an orphanage living under terrible conditions. Later, as an adult, he learned that the full translation of this verse is 'I will not leave you as orphans in the storm.' Of course, this had great meaning for Sterling's grandfather."

"And it must have really said something to you that day," Hope noted.

"Let me tell you the whole story," Carol continued. "Jesus and his followers had gone for a boat ride on the Sea of Galilee when a terrible storm blew up. Jesus lay down in the hull of the boat and took a nap. He was sound asleep as the boat began pitching and tossing on the angry sea. His followers were terrified."

"Jesus was sleeping through the storm!" Hope was startled.

"Interesting twist in the story," Carol agreed. "Obviously he was completely secure while the rest of the men were terrified. He knew about omnipresence and had a complete trust in the presence of God. His disciples woke him up, and when Jesus rebuked the storm, the sea became calm again. Of course, his followers were amazed at his ability to control nature. But Sterling helped me see a point to the story that will help anyone living through a storm. Why was Jesus so completely secure?"

"He trusted God?"

"True," Carol affirmed, "but Sterling saw something more concrete than believing the right ideas. Jesus demonstrated God's presence with them right in the middle of the storm. Omnipresence means that God is with us in both the good and bad times. The disciples didn't need to be afraid because Jesus was with them. If they had simply trusted in him, they wouldn't have had the flip-flops when fear was turning them inside out. You understand what this message means?"

"He is *truly* with us," Hope answered. "Omnipresence is much larger than an idea. And that's what helped you so much?"

"Definitely! I certainly knew what it was like to be lost in the tempest. I felt like my boat was sinking."

"You make my problems seem pretty small," the young woman said apologetically. "I've been worried about happiness while you had to face a terrible wound to your soul."

"A storm is a storm," Carol explained. "When we're hit by the lightning, it doesn't make any difference if the thunder sounds louder somewhere else. Here's what helped me the most. Sterling said that many people think that God is with them during the good times but gone when the hurricanes come."

"Sure. That's the way I've always thought."

"And that was Sterling's point. We won't have serenity until we are able to believe that God is with us regardless of the circumstances."

"That's what omnipresence means—we are never left as orphans in the storm?"

"Excellent! You've got it."

Hope sat back in her chair and pondered what she had been hearing. Carol's explanations sounded easy enough to grasp, but the implications were so big.

"Perhaps the starting point for me is to be able to write, 'I believe God is with me in my storm.'"

"That's where my fifteen-second convictions began." Carol patted Hope's hand. "I must tell you that believing in omnipresence has truly revolutionized my emotional life. I don't live with fear and confusion any longer."

"That's what you thought that afternoon?" Hope asked.

"I didn't know what to think. You've met the postman. He's not a psychiatrist, a priest, or a minister. His approach seemed really presumptuous. Yet I had this feeling that he not only knew what I felt and was there because he cared, but he also knew that blaming God had not filled the terrible void in me. So I mumbled something to the effect that I appreciated his concern, shook their hands, and walked them to the door."

"After they were gone, I went back to the kitchen table and stared at what he had written: 'I believe God loves me and he loved little Linda too. I believe he's hearing my prayer right now and that he feels my loss and pain even more deeply than I. I believe he will help me through this nightmare. And when I come out on the other side, I believe he will be the reason. My responsibility is to love and trust God regardless of what happens.'"

When Carol stopped, the young woman asked timidly, "And did you come out on the other side?"

"At first I didn't think that I could." Carol shook her head. "I don't need to tell you how hard it was. But I kept thinking about omnipresence. I began to realize that God was with me even when the evil was happening. He was also with my child in that terrible moment. While I can't understand all that he is doing at any given time, I can believe that nothing will keep him from loving and working for our good in all circumstances. I had to do whatever he wanted me to do."

"And when did that become clear to you?" Hope leaned forward.

"Later that night I couldn't sleep. I got up and came down to the table again. This time I started writing on the sheet entitled 'God wants me to . . .' I scribbled several lines before I faced the toughest part, but finally I wrote, 'God wants me to forgive Linda's killer.'

"I carried that piece of paper around with me for a long time before I faced up to what I knew I had to do. I eventually wrote to the man who killed my daughter. I sent a letter to the prison and forgave him for what he had done. And I've been able to see his wife and family several times to try to help them."

"I don't know what to say." The young seeker shook her head. "I don't see how you had the strength to do those things."

"When you do what you believe God wants you to do," Carol explained, "special assistance is added to your efforts."

"H-m-m . . ." the young woman pondered her answer.

"I had always been a good person," Carol added. "I did community volunteer work, and I went to church. I just didn't think anything as terrible as losing my daughter could happen to me.

"But the Book tells us that the rain falls on the just and the unjust (Matt. 5:45). A drunk is as liable to hit a sweet, innocent child as a bad person."

"You spoke of convictions, Carol. What did you learn from your ordeal?"

"I learned that God is bigger than anything he permits to happen. While life always involves some degree of suffering, God is bigger than all of it. He does help us to handle our problems. It's an inner miracle.

"Sterling Veteran also had me read this paragraph every day as I tried to decide how to complete those two statements: 'I believe God . . .' and 'God wants me to . . .' I read, 'In all these things we are more than conquerors through Him who loved us. For I am persuaded that neither death nor life, nor angels nor principalities nor powers, nor things present nor things to come, nor height nor depth, nor any other created thing, shall be able to separate us from the love of God' (Rom. 8:37–39)."

"You certainly have a powerful faith," Hope affirmed.

"But I didn't at the time of our tragedy. I discovered that I didn't have a great deal of faith, and I wasn't able to tackle one problem. Sterling showed me that we must face our problems with the amount of faith we have. Then, as we live through the disaster, our faith grows."

"What an important insight," Hope mused.

"Several weeks after I lost my daughter, an important memory came back to my mind. Just one week before Linda's death, I went with her to a youth gathering at a local church. The speaker was one of those spiritual jock types that the teens love. This human dynamo was talking about the story of David and Goliath."

"Gee," the young seeker laughed, "I haven't heard that story in years."

"The young man was quite a speaker," Carol continued. "He graphically described the enormity of the giant and how small the shepherd boy was. I was terrified even though I knew how the story ended. But then he drove his point home. The only real issue in their battle that day was that God was bigger than Goliath. Omnipresence was David's secret of success. His God was the unseen presence on the battlefield."

"How interesting! I wouldn't have thought of that twist in the story."

"Naturally I hoped that Linda was listening. But the week after her death, I suddenly realized that the young man was actually speaking to me. I was the one who needed to know that my heavenly Father was bigger than any of my problems. In a message for young people, God was preparing me to face my daughter's death even before it happened. I needed to know that God was even larger than the completely unsolvable issue of her death."

"You've certainly given me a great deal to think about," the seeker acknowledged. "I can't imagine finding serenity in the midst of such crushing circumstances."

"In fifteen seconds I have the recurring choice of remembering that I believe that God is working in the midst of every circumstance or of succumbing to the fear that life has no meaning or purpose," Carol told Hope. "Yes, there were times when I didn't want to live. I didn't want to face the future without my little Linda, but I knew that God would be with me. My convictions that he was and would be there allowed me to recognize that he could use what he did not cause, that he could make something good out of my pain."

"So . . . none of us can control whether the news is good or bad," the sincere young woman reflected, "but we can choose what we will believe about the problem."

"A fifteen-second choice," Carol noted. "Let me suggest," she continued, "that you talk further with someone who can add another important dimension to these convictions. Did Sterling give you Dr. Climber's name?"

"Yes."

"I think you ought to talk with him next." Carol Singer stood and offered her hand. "If I can be of further help, let me know. Remember to practice applying your fifteen-second convictions rather than stewing over bad news."

"I'm on my way," the seeker said over her shoulder as she walked down the driveway. "Thank you for your time and help."

She got in the car and looked at the address of Dr. Cliff Climber. Then she began to jot down her recollection of what Carol Singer had told her.

Here's what the younger seeker learned:

Fifteen-Second Convictions: Summary

1. *Remember omnipresence:* Whether calm or stormy, God is always here.

2. Write my major problem out on a piece of paper.

3. Write beneath that summary, "I believe God . . ." Then summarize what I know to be true about God in relation to my problem in less than one hundred words.

4. Then write out, "God wants me to . . ." Conclude by describing the kind of action God wants me to take.

5. At the point of painful memories practice fifteen-second reflections that God's love is working in the midst of every circumstance. Maintain the conviction that special assistance comes to those who do it his way.

6. *Remember:* 1. He will not leave me desolate!
               2. God is bigger than the giants in my life.

THREE _____

Fifteen-Second
Petitions

When Hope left Carol
Singer, she was genuinely moved. Fifteen-second convictions certainly made a lot of sense and challenged her.

Carol Singer had used her faith to help her face one of
life's most difficult problems. And the manner in which
she not only stated her convictions but searched for their
application made a lot of sense too. Her beliefs weren't
just ideas. Writing "God wants me to . . ." and then coming up with the appropriate action had helped her to face
problems more effectively.

But was that enough in itself? Surely there was more to
serenity than writing out one's problems, convictions,
and actions. Hope Moore wondered what Dr. Cliff

Climber would have to add. When she called and asked for an appointment, she was given a time only two days away.

When the young seeker walked in, Dr. Cliff Climber's office was filled with children and their parents. For a moment her heart sank; she would probably only have five minutes or less. Nonetheless, Hope went up to the receptionist's window and identified herself. The receptionist smiled and said, "Have a seat. Dr. Climber will be with you shortly."

Hope sighed. She had heard that from physicians' receptionists before. Her appointment could take anywhere from fifteen minutes to as long as two hours! Hope picked up a magazine and had just opened it when a nurse opened a door and said, "Dr. Climber will see you now." Hope was impressed.

The nurse led her to Dr. Climber's private office and suggested she have a seat. Once the door was closed, Hope began looking at the walls lined with pictures and Dr. Climber's medical degrees. In addition to pictures of his family, several seemed to show him in humanitarian service overseas. One particularly caught Hope's eye. In the middle of the picture was the postman helping Dr. Climber examine a little boy.

When the door opened, Dr. Climber entered and extended his hand. Rather than going behind his desk, he took the chair opposite her. She quickly scanned his demeanor. He was pleasant but obviously very busy. Even so, he quickly put her at ease.

"I'm glad you could come and that you were on time. That helps me very much. I've blocked out the next twenty minutes. Should we need more time, we can schedule another session."

The young seeker expressed her thanks and said that twenty minutes should be more than enough.

Dr. Climber continued. "I hear you're searching for the secret of serenity. You've talked to my postman and to Carol Singer as well. I practice the fifteen-second secret too. So tell me, what can I do to help?"

No time for small talk, Hope thought. "Carol told me she practices fifteen-second convictions. Since I haven't heard of this approach, I was hoping you could add more insight."

Dr. Climber nodded his head in agreement. "Of course, fifteen-second convictions are important, and they do work. I practice them myself."

"You do? You write out your convictions the way Mrs. Singer does?" Hope could envision Mrs. Singer taking the time more easily than a busy physician with all his problems.

Dr. Climber anticipated her question. "I'm a busy person. You're really wondering how I work in the reflection time, aren't you?"

"Yes, I guess so. For someone who has so many patients and such demands on his schedule, it seems unusual to plan your work in relation to your convictions."

Dr. Climber nodded again. "You're right. However, I've found that I can't afford not to write out my fifteen-second convictions. They are the necessary foundation for my fifteen-second petitions."

"Oh no!" she frowned quizzically. "Fifteen-second what?"

Dr. Climber smiled. "You heard right. Fifteen-second petitions. I apply the omnipotence of God."

"That's the third word the postman told me I needed to learn. What do you mean?"

"Most simply put . . ." Dr. Climber tapped his pencil on the desk and went on. "Omnipotence means unlimited authority and power. As a doctor who deals with life and death crises every day, I know how critical it can be to have real power behind you. Fifteen-second petitions draw on that reserve."

The young seeker shook her head. "First, it was a fifteen-second serenity, then fifteen-second convictions, and now fifteen-second petitions. Please do explain."

"Sure. A petition is a request to someone in authority. Since I'm applying convictions that are based on the ultimate Authority, I ask him to give me the special assistance I need."

"How does special assistance work?"

"It's really quite simple. Did you see my waiting room when you came in?"

She nodded and said, "Yes."

"It's like that every day. And when a virus hits, it's worse. We schedule patients weeks and even months in advance. Plus, I have hospital rounds to make on my way home, and once home, I usually get several telephone calls. Each morning I make rounds again before I come to the office. And of course there are always emergencies at the most unexpected times.

"Before I met Sterling Veteran, I tried to have special times of meditation. But they were always interrupted. I was usually so tired or preoccupied that I didn't feel my petitions were effective."

As Hope nodded her understanding, Dr. Climber continued. "Now, though, I'm able to petition constantly throughout the day. Praying 'on the hoof' is a part of the fifteen-second secret."

"How did you come to that idea?" she asked.

"Did you notice the picture of the postman and me overseas in Kenya?"

"I saw it first thing."

"I began to see that periodically Sterling seemed to be thinking very deeply about something. One day, I asked him, 'Hey! Where are you?' And he told me about fifteen-second petitions. Here's the idea: Though my days are packed, even on the busiest of days I find that I always have a few minutes when I'm not doing anything—sometimes between patients or telephone calls, sometimes when I'm going to the car, walking from the parking lot to the hospital, or making rounds. As the postman explained, we can break those times into fifteen-second segments. During the first fifteen seconds, I recall one of my convictions."

With that he reached over to his desk and pulled a card out of a box. "The first thing I do in the morning is pull out a Scripture card and read it. Then I put it in my pocket and carry it around with me all day. Every time I have a spare minute, I reach in and read this card." Dr. Climber leaned back in his chair and asked, "Would you like me to give you a very simple example?"

"Certainly," she replied.

"Well, the other day I pulled out a card that said, 'Casting all your care upon Him, for He cares for you' (1 Pet. 5:7). I read it, put it in my shirt pocket, made my hospital rounds, and came to the office.

"In the middle of the day, I needed to make an emergency run to the hospital, and I couldn't find my car keys. I was very frustrated. When my search didn't produce the keys, I thought about petitioning to find them.

My immediate response was that I shouldn't bother God with this irritation. Then I remembered my card from that morning. I pulled it out and read it again. My keys were a real care and concern because I was needed at the hospital. Then I breathed a small prayer, 'Please let me find my keys.'

"I buzzed my nurse and told her my problem. She looked around and said, 'Don't you usually leave them here on the desk?' I said, 'Yes.' She walked around my desk and noticed the trash. 'Have you looked in the trash?' she asked. I hadn't, but there were my keys. Maybe if I had called my nurse first, I wouldn't have needed to read my card. Or maybe the card helped me to think to call my nurse. Either way it was a fifteen-second way of casting my cares on him."

"Finding your keys sure helped."

"Of course," he agreed. "But that's not really the point. Rather than become completely frustrated, I had a quick way of dealing with my tension that kept me from ending up in complete turmoil."

Hope smiled and commented, "That's the fifteen-second hit again."

"Sure. Now let me tell you what I do with the next fifteen seconds. I thank him for his love. I tell him how much I appreciate the fact that he operates this world out of compassion and concern for us and in particular for me. Focusing my mind on such a constructive under-standing of life really keeps me from slipping over into despair and fear. Fear is the most significant enemy we have to fight."

"Really?" Hope frowned. "Why do you believe such a thing?"

Dr. Cliff Climber leaned back in his chair and for a moment was lost in his own reflections. "Viruses come and go, but there's no infection so hard to fight as fear. In a split second, the fright disease rushes through your blood stream into your brain and then shoots through your whole endocrine system, throwing everything into a total panic. Fear grips the body, locking your muscles up tight. A shot of penicillin can kill a bug, but no one has the injection to stop fear."

"Wow!" Hope shook her head. "That's right!"

"Several years ago I had one of those experiences every physician dreads. An anesthesiologist made a mistake, and my patient suffered some severe consequences. Her family sued both of us.

"I was terribly depressed. I hadn't done anything wrong, and yet I was a part of what went on. The week before the case went to court, I was searching for some clue as to how I was going to survive. As God would have it, on the Sunday morning before the trial, my pastor preached a sermon about an ancient king. The text was from 1 Samuel 17:47, 'The battle is the LORD's.'

"Sitting in that church, I began to think of my mother," the physician smiled. "Of course, all of us have special places in our hearts for our mothers. But one of my mom's unusual qualities came to mind as I listened to that sermon. She was a living picture of patience."

"Sitting tight," Hope interrupted, "has never been my long suit. I'm all ears."

"Not mine either," the doctor agreed, "but fortunately I had Christian parents of the fifteen-second variety. My mother lived by the verse

> But those who wait on the LORD
> Shall renew their strength . . .
> They shall run and not be weary,
> They shall walk and not faint (Isa. 40:31).

Many times I saw that promise renew her. During a crisis she became very quiet, closed her eyes, and simply sat still until something important was transacted in her spirit. When she opened her eyes, she was like a great eagle taking to the skies."

"That example must have been very reassuring to you as a child," Hope reflected.

"I knew there wasn't anything that she and God couldn't do. She believed that he was in control, and she was quite willing to wait until she got his marching orders. As I listened to that Sunday morning sermon, I remembered her confidence that ultimately everything would work out. I kept seeing her trusting face."

"I'm sure that those words became flesh in her," Hope responded. "We all need to see ideas take shape in people. You 'fifteen-second' Christians have done that for me."

"I was thinking of her as the minister continued to repeat the phrase, 'the battle is the LORD's.' The setting for the story was an ancient battle between Israel and the nations of Ammon and Moab. The Hebrew king at that time was named Jehoshaphat. The Bible clearly says that he was afraid, but he began to make petitions calling on God for help. While the King was seeking divine intervention, a prophet appeared who told him to trust that 'the battle is the LORD's.' So the king had a fifteen-second decision to make. Either he would let fear control him, or he would have faith in the message from God."

"What happened?" Hope asked eagerly.

"The king and his men rose very early in the morning

and went out to fight. However, as they prepared to face their life-and-death conflict, the king sent a choir in front of the army singing praises to God. In the thick of the showdown, it sounded like Sunday morning worship."

"Must have been strange."

"What followed was far more amazing. Apparently their enemies became confused, walked into an ambush, and ended up killing each other. Afterward the king walked through the battle scene collecting the cattle and spoils of war that had been left behind. God's omnipotence had been demonstrated."

"What an awesome story!"

"We all have times," Dr. Climber explained, "when we don't know what to do except trust God. That's when our extremity becomes his opportunity. The one who created the universe still lives in the human heart, which is the real battleground. So as I kept hearing the minister's words—'the battle is the Lord's'—I realized that if I turned the issues over to him, the problems weren't mine anymore. They were God's concern. The future wasn't in the hands of the judge, the lawyers, or the insurance companies."

"What happened to you?" Hope's eyes widened.

"We won the case, but the real story is what happened to me before I even stepped into the courthouse." Cliff smiled broadly. "The significant verdict was the one rendered in my spirit. I knew that regardless of any legal action, God was in control. Winning the battle with fear was the true victory. I could see all of my little everyday trials as simple exercises in learning to trust God regardless of what is around or within us. I came to a new plateau in my ability to face any problem. My mother's faith became mine for the first time."

"What a wonderful discovery!" Hope exclaimed.

"From that time forward, I pray daily about every problem I face. Fifteen seconds make all the difference in the world," Cliff beamed. "Fear dissolves when I make my petitions."

"You are certainly filling in the blank places," she smiled. "What about the other fifteen-second segments?"

"I pray for my neighbor. Sometimes that's a patient I've just seen; other times, it's for a part of the world where disaster has struck. But I spend those seconds praying for someone else by name.

"And finally I pray for wisdom to make accurate diagnoses, that I'll not neglect my family—all kinds of things. But I pray for me for at least fifteen seconds, several times each day."

The young seeker was impressed. "I've never heard of a praying doctor."

Dr. Climber smiled. "To tell you the truth, I don't know how I made it as a physician before. Many times my patients expect so much of me that I feel terribly inadequate. I know that I'm only a human being trained in medicine, not a miracle worker. That's when my fifteen-second prayers become my lifeline to sanity and stability. And I often suddenly feel an inner peace. Of course, that's the payoff you're seeking."

Silence fell between them. Dr. Climber stood. "Well, I hope I haven't disappointed you."

Hope scrambled to her feet. "Oh, no. It's all so new that I really don't know what to say."

"I have patients I need to see, but I think there's another person on our postman's route with whom you ought to visit."

The young woman's eye was distracted by one of the pictures on the wall. "Is the person in this picture?"

"No," he answered, "but she's doing something every bit as important. Her name is Mercy Carrier and she's a schoolteacher."

The young seeker's eyes dropped. *A schoolteacher?* she thought. *Why not someone like Dr. Climber?*

"Now, don't look disappointed," Dr. Climber chided Hope. "She's probably one of the most incredibly serene and fulfilled people I've ever met. If you want to know how to practice fifteen-second effectiveness, I couldn't direct you to a better person."

He went to his desk and pulled out a sheet of paper on which he wrote Mercy Carrier's name and telephone number. As he gave it to Hope, he said, "You have a great surprise in store for you."

"I'll look forward to meeting her. And thanks so much for your time and for telling me about your fifteen-second petitions."

The sincere young woman got into her car and sat quietly. For the first time since she had begun her search, the confidence that she was making progress energized and excited her. She was really anticipating her visit to Mercy Carrier.

Hope's incredible journey began with a postman and continued with a homemaker, then a physician, and now a teacher. The path was so different from what she had imagined as she began her quest. She had always thought it would end in an esoteric seminar, a set of books, or an expenditure of money to a great teacher or saint who would open up hidden secrets. Instead, her discoveries had been with the most ordinary people of all. And it hadn't occurred in some great gathering or motivational seminar, but in homes and a doctor's office. She smiled at her naïveté.

When arrived at home, she immediately went to the phone. A pleasant voice answered, and Mercy seemed to know that she would be calling. Within seconds she had an appointment to visit Mercy Carrier at her school. Hope couldn't wait. But before she left home she added her new insights to her growing journal:

Fifteen-Second Petitions: Summary

1. *Remember: omnipotence.* God has all authority and power.

2. Start praying "on the hoof" as soon as any need arises.

3. Practice praying in sixty-second units divided into fifteen-second segments.

   a. Select a Bible verse to be recalled in the first fifteen seconds.

   b. Make a fifteen-second petition for my pressing problem.

   c. Use fifteen seconds to thank God for his care for you.

   d. Spend fifteen seconds petitioning for family, friends, neighbors, and needs around the world.

4. *Remember:* The battle is the Lord's. He has the power to put the pieces back together in a new and creative way.

FOUR _____

Fifteen-Second Practicing

The seeker entered Central High School and asked for directions to Mercy Carrier's classroom, which she easily found. After they had introduced themselves, Mercy Carrier went immediately to the point: "I hear you're wanting to know more about how to apply the fifteen-second secret of serenity."

The sincere young woman smiled. "That's right."

"Well, how's your search going?"

"Since I met the postman, things are going great—but I'm still trying to grasp his fifteen-second concept. When Carol Singer talked about fifteen-second convictions and Dr. Climber described fifteen-second petitions, the ideas really blew my mind!"

Mercy Carrier nodded understandingly. "The approach is certainly different. But the important thing is that it works, especially fifteen-second practicing."

"What? Here we go again. What in the world is *that?*" The young seeker shook her head.

"Sounds strange," Mercy agreed, "but it is an important part of a sense of well-being. We can't find peace of mind by only thinking about ourselves all of the time. We have to be of value to others."

"Now that's a new twist!" The seeker was pensive. "Most of what I have read has been about self-fulfillment, self-realization, self-discovery, self-development, selfhood, and on and on. Peace of mind was based on getting the most for yourself."

"Fifteen-second practicing turns those philosophies around. The question isn't what I can get but what I can give."

"Please describe what you mean."

"Our society puts a premium on accumulating," Mercy explained. "I know because I teach government and sociology. We glamorize people who become wealthy and amass fortunes, but we don't idolize selfless, nameless practitioners of kindness."

Hope Moore shook her head. "Sure. I grew up in the world of yuppies. I have to admit that most of my quest has been self-centered."

"Our built-in need to survive naturally causes us to be concerned with our own well-being," Mercy explained as she offered a chair to Hope. "We don't need to feel bad about healthy self-interest. But, happiness can't be found when we are stuck on ourselves. We must reach out to others if we are ever going to find serenity."

"How did you come to that conclusion?"

"Our mutual friend, the fifteen-second Christian, got

me started reading the Bible. Of course, I read the stories about Jesus. As I did so, I began to notice a very interesting thing. Jesus was continually touching people."

"Touching? Why would that be significant?" Hope was puzzled.

"Let me tell you one of the stories that I read in Matthew's Gospel." Mercy settled back in her chair. "Jesus was walking down the road when a leper came up asking him for help. He wanted to be healed. Do you know anything about lepers?"

"Only that the disease is horrible—the flesh sloughs off and leaves hideous sores."

"In addition," Mercy added, "lepers are complete social outcasts. People would do anything to avoid contact with them. Jesus would have naturally avoided such a man. Right?"

"Certainly."

"Wrong. He didn't," Mercy smiled. "In fact, Matthew tells us that the first thing that Jesus did when he saw the man was reach out and touch him. By doing so, he was violating every health code of his day."

"What are you driving at?" Hope asked.

"The leper had lost all dignity and personal worth. He was so far down the social ladder that he was untouchable. By first reaching out and touching the man, Jesus restored his dignity and self-worth before he did anything about the man's illness. In that touch, Jesus conveyed God's unconditional love at the man's point of greatest need—to be accepted back into society."

"That's a remarkable insight," the seeker replied. "And you try to do the same thing?"

"In fifteen seconds I have the possibility of making a difference in how someone feels about himself. Touching is a very practical way to express caring. When I give away my affection, I receive well-being in return."

Hope Moore rubbed her chin. "And that's fifteen-second practicing? Does a school teacher do that?"

Mercy Carrier pointed to the room. "I teach five classes of high school English with about thirty students in each class. That's 150 kids. I love every one of them, but each one is so unique. They are from such different backgrounds, and their behavior is outrageous at times. Despite the fact that I see them every day, five days a week, I seldom have time to visit with them for an extended period. That's why fifteen-second practicing made such a difference."

"I've already learned that our convictions play a major role in our finding peace in the midst of chaos," the young woman interjected, "but how could you practice your beliefs with all of these students?"

"Let me be completely honest." Mercy crossed her arms. "Some people are much more difficult to love than are others. I have some kids who are so motivated that they always do more than is asked of them. Other students are simply one big mess . . . never getting anything in on time. Of course, they're frustrating. But I've developed a fresh perspective on all of them based on the meaning of the love of God."

"The love of God?" Hope wrinkled her brow. "I never thought of schoolteaching as being about the love of God."

"Certainly. Every area of life is covered by his care and concern. God loves us equally. Jesus was as concerned for the leper as he would have been for a socially prominent leader. He reminded us that the rain falls both on the just and the unjust. So I have found a way of conveying his care and concern regardless of the behavior of my students or friends. Through fifteen-second practicing I've found an ideal way to tell each person that he is important. I learned the method from the story of Jesus and the leper."

"How in the world can you do such a thing?" Hope threw up her hands.

"With my hands—" Mercy pointed at Hope's gesture. "I'm constantly aware of students and even colleagues who need a touch. I never hesitate to give one."

"A touch?" she nodded. "So fifteen-second practicing is touching people?"

"Touching is part of it because it's very important that people be affirmed," she answered. "Psychiatrists have found that every human being has skin hunger. We crave a tender touch. The contact is never more than a touch on the hand or a shoulder—or maybe just a handshake. But touching is important."

"Exactly how does this work, Mrs. Carrier?"

"I look them right in the eye. It's surprising how many people never make direct contact. Then I tell them in a specific way that they are appreciated. I don't just make some general comment. That's too hazy. I find something that I can specifically affirm as I touch them."

The young seeker stopped her. "But you have 150 or so students. Surely you can't go around touching, looking them in the eye, and affirming each of them personally."

Mrs. Carrier agreed. "That's true—although you would be surprised how many you can affirm when you're intentional about it."

"Because you are their teacher, I know that must be extremely important to them. And you can do all that in fifteen seconds?"

"That's the model: touching, contact, and affirmation," said Mercy Carrier. "For example, I have each stu-
dent turn in at least one written assignment every two
weeks or so. Their projects are a point of contact. When I
grade those papers, I do two things: First, I try to be very
clear about the mistakes they made. Second, I then take
time to make a point about their good qualities, their
personhood, and their value as human beings. When they
read what I have said, I am touching them.

"My kids feel a lot of insecurity; they're bewildered.
Leaving home soon, getting a job, going to college, getting married—all these leave teenagers bewildered and
feeling unprepared. They need clear and direct guidance
and even discipline when necessary. But they also need
affirmation and love.

"On each paper, I take at least fifteen seconds to write
an affirming message to them. I've been doing it so long
that they would feel I was angry with them if I didn't. I
really think they know that I like them, that I'm for
them, and that I want them to do their very best. As a
result, I have a high achievement level in my classes."

"I'm impressed," the young woman answered, "but
how can you find something to write about for 150 kids?"

Mercy said, "Because I make it a point to reach out. I
have their behavior and class participation to write
about, their attitude, their work, plus the paper I have
before me. And I write a note to anyone who doesn't
hand in an assignment as well."

"I'm trying to imagine all the work you must do," the
young woman sighed. "Sure adds a lot to your teaching
load. That's really incredible! Now I understand why Dr.
Climber was so enthusiastic about you and the things you
do. But what if you weren't a teacher? How would

fifteen-second practicing apply then? The way he talked, you're involved in many other pursuits."

"Dr. Cliff Climber is a dear friend and may have overstated my accomplishments. I do work in the community. Dr. Climber and I have worked together at the Good Samaritan Shelter for neglected children."

"He didn't mention that project."

"Well, he really does a lot of similar services in the community as well as the overseas volunteer medical work."

"I'm stunned," Hope admitted. "I didn't know there were still people like the two of you left."

"Sure, there are a lot of us fast-moving peace pursuers out there," Mercy laughed. "Mother Teresa once said that Christ often appears to us in the most disgusting disguises. I see him everywhere I go, but especially with the children at the Good Samaritan Shelter. It's one of the most meaningful outlets for my fifteen-second practicing."

"There must be a difference," the young woman interjected, "between fifteen-second practicing with abused children and with your high school students?"

"Yes and no. Since the shelter children have been damaged, we can't expect them to respond initially to normal acts of care. Sometimes they're afraid of being touched, while other times they seem desperate for contact. Regardless, I always look lovingly into their eyes. Gradually, I'm able to establish enough confidence that they want to be touched and held. They are so incredibly hungry for genuine affirmation and appreciation! I always find something very positive and concrete to point out to them. Even with neglected children, it's possible to do a lot of good in fifteen seconds.

"Now and then situations that arise take a much greater investment of time. Just a few weeks ago, one very significant example occurred. Did you notice the small boy leaving when you entered?"

"The one with black hair and a red sweater?"

"That's Ernest Walker. He had a terrible problem with self-esteem and always sat in the back of the class. He seldom participated even when I called on him. He simply didn't think he had anything to offer."

The seeker rolled her eyes. "How I remember the pain of high school. I wouldn't be a teenager again for a million dollars."

"I didn't treat Ernest like a loser. I checked with the counselor, and they found that he had almost no home life. His parents are divorced, and his mother works evenings. Somewhere along the way, life turned sour on my little friend.

"I was determined that Ernest Walker would never feel inept in my class. When he turned in his papers, I always found a way to say something good about what he had done. When he didn't turn one in, I gave him a paper back with a statement that I knew he could do it; he only needed to try. Then one day he dawdled around so that he would be the last one to leave the room. Noticing that he was lingering, I put my hand on his shoulder and asked him how he was doing. He mumbled something that I couldn't understand. Finally, he looked up and asked a question that cut right through me. He said, 'Mrs. Carrier, why do you pay so much attention to me?'

"I couldn't help myself. I reached over and put my arms around him. I said his name and told Ernest that I cared for him, not because I was his English teacher but because he was special."

"That must have been very important to him," the young woman observed.

"He looked stunned for a moment; then he said, 'Why? I'm a nobody.'

"'Ernest,' I told him, 'I've learned a wonderful fact about both of us. We are very important people even when we forget the fact. God's love has given me great worth, and he wants me to pass the same value on to you. I've been accepted in order to be able to offer the same acceptance to you. In the eyes of God, you are truly *somebody*.'"

"He must have been amazed," Hope observed.

"Ernest told me that I seemed to care more than his own family did. I told him that sometimes people just haven't found out how important they are to God and that keeps them from passing on the good news to others. Other students were coming in for the next hour, and I knew he would be embarrassed in front of them. So I asked him to come see me after school. When he did, he opened up and told his painful story."

Mercy Carrier shook her head. "What parents do to their children is just beyond me."

"Don't stop now," urged Hope. "I want to know what became of Ernest."

"During the weeks that followed I went out of my way to treat him as a person of supreme value. I asked him questions in class and then listened to whatever he said as if he were a scholar of renown. I pointed out the value of his comments to the class. Quickly their attitudes toward him changed. They listened when he talked. I went to other teachers and asked them to join me in an effort I nicknamed Project: Human Worth. I told them that I was trying to restore this young man's self-esteem, and I solicited their help. We didn't give him any extra breaks, but simply treated him as a person with a worth that he had never owned. I asked my colleagues to touch him with their personal concern."

"The other teachers cooperated?"

"Yes, they know something about the secret too. Touching lives takes a little more time, but it brings a lot more satisfaction."

"Has Ernest really changed?" the sincere young woman probed.

"Incredibly! Our concern has made a total change in him. He's turning in his assignments and even volunteers to answer a question occasionally. And it all started with fifteen-second practicing.

"I find it crucial to be alert on a daily basis to providing helpful acts of love and concern, even for fifteen seconds. They not only add up to hours and days of involvement, but they can have a lifetime impact."

The young seeker was very impressed. Moving forward in her chair she said, "I never knew grading papers could be a source of fulfillment, but I do now."

Mercy Carrier added, "Not just grading papers, but anything we do."

Hope nodded her agreement. "You've given me an extraordinary way to approach fifteen-second practicing."

"I must run on to my next class." Mrs. Carrier stood up. "But I have a colleague who can share some other helpful insights into how we find serenity while teaching wild and crazy high school kids. Most people wouldn't believe it was possible."

"I certainly wouldn't have," the seeker agreed.

"Earlier I asked Dusty Rhoades to drop by and chat. You'll find him to be a very interesting person. I think that he's the only serene basketball coach in the world—certainly the only one I know. Ask him what he thinks about the fifteen-second approach. He'll be here in just a moment."

"Thank you so much for your time." Hope extended her hand. Mercy Carrier reached out instead and took her shoulder. She squeezed it lightly for a moment and looked into Hope's eyes. "Your interest has encouraged me to keep on practicing another day. What a helpful person you are."

Suddenly Mercy was gone into the hall crowded with students changing classes. Hope Moore stood there for a moment enjoying how good this teacher had made her feel. "Heavens!" she suddenly exclaimed. "I've just been the recipient of fifteen-second practicing. I must write down what I've heard so I don't forget a word."

Here is what the young seeker wrote:

Fifteen-Second Practicing: Summary

1. *Remember:* Serenity comes from what I give—not what I get.

2. Touching is a simple, effective way to express caring.

3. Fifteen-second practicing involves a touch. Maybe it's just a pat on the shoulder, a squeeze on the arm, or a handshake.

4. Look the person you're practicing on right in the eye, and maintain eye contact while talking to him.

5. Always find something *very* specific that you can affirm and express your appreciation for.

6. Do this procedure in fifteen seconds or less.

7. *Remember:* People are different, but God equally loves all of them.

FIVE _____

Fifteen-Second Applications

Hope extended her hand. "A serene basketball coach?" she asked.

"Hey, don't judge a book by its cover," the tall handsome young man in the letter sweater quipped as he shook hands. "Nothing goes better with competition than a little peace of mind afterward."

"Well, that's more bounce to the ounce."

"Absolutely. I'm Dusty Rhoades."

"What a pleasure to meet you. I'm Hope Moore. I'm here to find out how people like you and Mercy Carrier live such composed lives."

"You've hit our favorite subject. We all use the fifteen-second secret to make the world a better and happier place. What can I tell you?"

"Mercy Carrier has been instructing me on fifteen-second practicing. Could you tell me a bit more?"

"Sure. What in particular would be the most helpful?"

"Both of you seem to find a great deal of satisfaction in your work. You know how to help others in ways that also help you. I'd like to know more about how you are able to do so much good for yourselves and others."

"As a basketball coach," Dusty said, taking off his sweater, "I know how important it is to find someone who can teach you how to really play the game." He laid the sweater on a chair. "So to prepare for the game of life I wanted a teacher who really knew what it was all about. Make sense?"

"Of course," the young seeker smiled. "I have been listening to some very good players. Sterling Veteran and Carol Singer introduced me to the rules of the game, and Cliff Climber told me about getting energized. Perhaps Mercy Carrier told me about making points."

"Very good," Dusty laughed. "You've got my drift."

"Now I'm ready for more coaching."

"And for that instruction," Dusty straddled his chair, "I think I've found the all-time winner. Although he lived a long time ago, the experts agree that he was unexcelled in maintaining serenity in the midst of both the best and the worst that life had to offer. He was known to everyone who heard him as the total teacher."

"The total teacher?"

Dusty nodded. "Yes. He talked about every area of life that really counted, and his solutions have stood the test of time. No one who has tried his way has ever been disappointed."

"Now that's a track record!"

"You've done it again," he laughed. "But what's

equally important is that the people he touched received a sense of peace that even the worst of circumstances couldn't destroy. Since he did that for his students, I want to know that I can do the same for mine."

"Me too," Hope agreed. "Tell me more."

"He lived in an obscure country that was occupied by a hostile army. Even though he was born in a poor home and came without significant credentials, once he started teaching, his fame spread far and wide. What he said was to become the basis of all Western civilization. I believe he is the most qualified teacher in all of history."

"Don't stop now. Who is this person?"

"His Hebrew name was Yeshua. In modern English we call him Jesus—Jesus of Nazareth."

"Sure," Hope answered. "Your friends have been talking about him."

"Of course, most people have heard about Jesus, but few understand how he brought serenity to those who listened to him. They fail to pick up on the clues that he demonstrated in his teaching."

"I don't understand," Hope frowned. "What do you mean?"

"Let me ask you a question." Dusty Rhoades pointed his finger at her. "Where did the total teacher teach?"

"I'm not an expert, but wasn't it in places like Galilee and Jerusalem?"

Dusty nodded his head in approval. "But wasn't there a need for what he was saying in Rome and Cairo—or Athens?"

"Well, yes, I'm sure there was," she replied thoughtfully. "But he wasn't in those places. He was in Israel. And transportation and communications weren't all that good."

"You're right," he said. "And when he was in Jerusalem, what about the people back in Nazareth and Samaria? Didn't they still have needs?"

"Well, yes—I mean, he was in a physical body and could be in only one place at a time."

"That's exactly my point. Jesus didn't leave Judea. He didn't even minister to everybody there. He reached out to those who came into *the scope of his awareness*."

The young seeker said, "What an interesting observation."

"Most of us spend most of our time holding out for a better day and a better place. But fifteen-second practicing begins by accepting this moment as the only one we will ever have. We start where we are."

Hope wrinkled her forehead. "Just being aware of what's at hand?"

"Yes." The coach gestured as if he were encouraging one of his players. "I got that insight from a very interesting story Sterling Veteran had me read. Jesus used the story to teach an affluent young man what life was really all about. Ever hear of the good Samaritan?"

Hope hesitated. "Well, only vaguely."

"Okay!" Dusty was enthusiastic. "The whole story started with a question from a lawyer who had everything except something money can't buy. He wanted to live forever. So he asked Jesus what it would take."

"I didn't know that's what prompted the story," Hope answered.

"Here's what's interesting," Dusty continued. "What the young attorney was asking about was how he could have life in such *quantity* that it would never end. But Jesus answered him by telling him how to have a heavenly *quality* of life starting right now."

"Wow!" She laughed. "That's amazing."

"Jesus used the story of the good Samaritan to demonstrate that people who help others will already be living such a wonderful life that they won't worry about living forever."

"So scope of awareness means seeing people in need?"

Dusty nodded. "But I'm talking about fifteen-second awareness. In that short fraction of a minute a decision is made either to help or to go on by. The story Jesus told described how the most important religious leaders and fellow countrymen of the injured man simply didn't pay attention to the injured man's pain. A foreigner who was considered an enemy was the only one to respond. They all took the same amount of time to say either yes or no!"

"So I need to develop the habit of instant response to the needs of others?" Hope asked.

"Yes, if we want to have a quality of life that is forever," Dusty confirmed. "I find that I am constantly surrounded by situations and people who could use a little help. I've already made up my mind that I'm going to be available. You know what? I'm the one who is always the happiest."

"I'm sure this school is filled with troubled people."

"Yes," Dusty slowly acknowledged, "but I'm not called on to take care of the whole school—just the ones who are in my scope of awareness. See the difference?"

"Yes," Hope answered. "A person could really get buried in trying to take care of the whole world. That wouldn't be a very serene existence!"

"One of my basketball boys was in trouble," Dusty drawled. "We called him Tom the traveler because he had the bad habit of running with the basketball. He also had a bad inclination with the wrong people. The traveler got into drugs. Most of the teachers wanted him out of the school system—and with good reason. But I saw the boy as my man in the ditch. I wasn't asked to make a judgment about why he'd gotten himself into trouble. I just knew he needed someone to help him get back to a place where he could get well. So I picked up the ole traveler and went to work on his problems. Today he's making the grade and is back on his way. We just start where we are."

"Yes," the young woman said slowly, "living in the now."

"And recognizing how important now is," Dusty added. "For years I didn't feel that being a coach was particularly important. I enjoyed sports, kids, and competition. Yet I didn't feel that what I did counted for much. When a game was over, I always felt a letdown, an emptiness about my life."

"Excitement is hard to sustain," the seeker noted.

"A coach knows the limits on the time that anyone can maintain enthusiasm. Life has to add up to a lot more than hype."

"That's for sure!"

"Now I'm playing in the game of life, and I know I'm making a difference that will last long after all the score cards have been counted. For example, I've been able to teach Tom how to stay out of trouble. Part of his problem was that he really didn't have any idea about how to handle temptations. He simply fell into one mess after another. If there was a decision to be made, he almost automatically chose the wrong alternative."

"He must have been in trouble all the time," Hope concluded.

"I had him memorize a very simple verse from the Bible. Remember this—the wrong desire that comes into your life isn't anything new and different. Many others have faced exactly the same problems before you. Ever hear this one? 'No temptation has overtaken you such as is common to man; but God is faithful, who will not allow you to be tempted beyond what you are able, but with the temptation will also make the way of escape, that you may be able to bear it' (1 Cor. 10:13). Is that new to you?'"

"Is it ever!" Hope grinned. "I suppose I've lived by the same philosophy that Oscar Wilde held. I think he said, 'The only way to get rid of a temptation is to yield to it.' I'm not that bad, but I never dreamed that there was really help to deal with our temptations."

"You'd be surprised about what the Bible teaches," Dusty countered.

"Yes," Hope said reluctantly, "I really don't know much about what you call the Christian life. I've heard some of the Bible stories, but I didn't know there was so much practical guidance for everyday living."

"This verse taught me fifteen-second resistance," Dusty continued. "I realized that most of my decisions about temptation were made in a quarter of a minute. I either was or I wasn't. It's that simple. Most of the rest of my thinking about moral issues was window dressing."

"How fascinating. Your fifteen-second secret has done it again."

"I helped Tom recognize how crucial it was to make immediate response when something bad or negative started tugging on his imagination. He could depend on the fact that somewhere directly in front of his eyes there was an escape hatch if he wanted to take it."

"I've certainly never looked for trouble," Hope said slowly, "but I can't say that I've had raving success in resisting problems that tug on my weaknesses. I wish I could do better."

"Temptation is normal," Dusty continued, "and none of us can avoid the problem. What counts is how quickly we face up to what's going on in our minds. I helped my ole buddy the traveler to recognize that the issue isn't the enticement but our immediate response. Don't worry with the magnetism. Resist mulling it over."

"Another new angle!" Hope snapped her fingers. "The idea certainly helps me, and you will probably never know how much you helped that boy." She added, "I can see how his whole life could be changed by that one idea. You certainly have a special feel for kids."

"I understand because I've been there." Dusty's voice was low and intense. "But for the grace of God, I would have stayed in the same hole that Tom was in. There was a time when I was set for the bright lights, and then I took a real fall."

"Dusty Rhoades . . ." Hope's hand came to her mouth. "Now I remember! You were an all-American basketball player."

"And I was on my way to the NBA when the door slammed in my face."

"A drug scandal!" Hope gasped. "It was in all the papers!"

"Pretty sad story," the coach sighed. "Really blew my life apart. I started taking steroids because I had this huge ego and would do anything to win. I had to be the best even if it meant cutting corners. Somewhere along the way I started doing drugs because they gave me a reprieve from my compulsive drive to be the big winner. Before I knew what had happened, I was hooked."

"How very sad. You must have gone through a great ordeal."

"No one really knew the full extent of my problem. In fact, I picked up the name Dusty from my drug usage. Ever hear of angel dust? I was really deeply into the stuff."

"What happened? How did you get out?"

"I had to face the fact that I had become a drug addict and admit it. Of course, the newspaper stories really put the heat on me. The good Book says, 'Pride goes before destruction' (Prov. 16:18). I had no recourse but to look my pride square in the eye and swallow hard. I took a long look at Dusty. What I saw made me face up to the sickness of always having to be the best. Drugs were only a secondary temptation. . . . The real problem was my need to be somebody big."

"Must have been a very hard time in your life."

"Yes," Dusty smiled, "but the pain of becoming honest turned me into a new person. If I hadn't faced up to the real temptation in my life, I would have never overcome my problems. Now I recognize that many times every day, I have a fifteen-second decision to make. Will I try to be big time, or will I settle for just being me? Will I let my fear of failure run my life, or will I recognize that there are people around me who need the same encouragement as I do to be significant? When I help them, I help myself."

"So that's where you got into fifteen-second resistance?"

"Right. Helping the Toms and Ernests on my teams is

far more important than winning. I had not realized how much good one single person can do."

"I think we all feel that way quite often," the sincere young woman replied.

"I thought unless you were an Albert Schweitzer, a Mother Teresa, or a Jonas Salk, you couldn't expect to make a lot of difference in the world. So real satisfaction and peace of mind were reserved for the chosen few."

"Obviously things have changed," Hope observed.

"I gave up the idea of going to India or Egypt to find opportunities for fulfillment. I let go of the notion that I needed to do some other sort of work to count. I quit holding out for another day and started concentrating on what was right under my nose.

"I began to look at my fellow teachers in a different light. Every one needed appreciation and affirmation. Teaching is tough business."

"A few simple words can sure make a difference," Hope added.

"Tremendous difference!" Dusty agreed. "I suppose Mercy gave you some examples of her special work with her students."

"She told me about Ernest."

"Good example. Every day I try to notice him. Chances are good that we are making the needed difference in his life."

Hope nodded her head in understanding. "Showing appreciation, grading papers, and writing notes of affirmation can be part of our scope of awareness, huh?"

"Yes," Dusty answered. "When anyone gives us full attention, we feel that we are being cared for."

"I certainly can't imagine," the seeker added, "that the total teacher didn't give his full attention to the people he was interacting with."

"It's like the preschool to which I take my little daughter," Dusty explained. "When I walk in, the teachers seem to ignore me. They kneel down in front of my little delight, smile, look her in the eye, and tell her how glad they are to see her. Then—and it's always second—they stand up and say 'Hello' to me. But they make sure that the person for whom that school is operating is greeted on her level and with full eye contact.

"I think the same should be true of our interaction with others. Expressing love and concern requires our full attention. We do that with our eyes."

The woman pursed her lips. "Sometimes such directness makes me feel uncomfortable."

"At first," Dusty agreed, "we may feel like we're getting too close. But I've found that I feel good about myself and what I'm saying when I go ahead and look the other person straight in the eye. In turn, good things happen to that other person emotionally."

"Then, what do I do next?"

"Well," Dusty continued, "we might try several approaches. What did Mercy suggest?"

"She said to find something positive and specific to say to the person we touch."

He agreed. "The important point is to be specific. Too many times people talk in a general way about how they feel toward others. Consequently, what they say comes off as insincere or unimportant. But a specific statement of appreciation avoids that."

The sincere young woman thought a minute. "I see

what you mean. But what if you don't know the person very well? Isn't it hard to find something specific?"

He shook his head. "At first, it may seem so, but really it's a matter of disciplining ourselves to be observant. We can become skilled at finding something affirming to say about every person we meet. In the context of fifteen-second practicing, our words can have a tremendous impact upon those with whom we come into contact."

"The key ingredient in making a difference is to confine your responses to fifteen seconds," Hope responded, "and not drag it out."

The coach reached over and placed his hand on Hope's shoulder. "That's excellent. You're very perceptive."

"You've made my day." The young woman beamed.

"Now just keep on practicing until the process is second nature. Ever take karate?"

"No, but I've watched people doing those strange exercises."

"Looks unusual, but those routines are the ultimate secret of success. Each ploy is practiced until it becomes habit—the athletes let their reflexes do all the work for them. Same thing happens with fifteen-second procedures. At first you may feel a little unnatural, but with time the life of faith just becomes second nature. That's when you really get the benefits."

"Thank you so much for all your help. I'll keep working, trying until I get it right."

"Well, it works." Dusty stood up and reached for his sweater. "I'm sorry but I have to grade some papers myself, so I must go. What's your next step?"

"I think it's time to go back and check in with the postman. I've learned a great deal, but there is a basic point that I need to check out with him. I certainly am learning about peace of mind."

"Remember," Dusty said, giving her a parting thought, "when you make someone else feel good, you are creating the climate in which you will find your own personal fulfillment. That's the secret of fifteen-second applications."

"I've got to get your instruction down." She took out her pencil as he waved good-bye. "Thank you so much for all of your help."

Here's what the young seeker added to her list:

Fifteen-Second Applications: Summary

1. *Remember:* Serenity comes to me as I give a sense of well-being to others.

2. Recognize and remember that I only have this one time and place in which to live. Don't wait for a better opportunity.

3. Practice expanding my scope of awareness. Pay attention to each person I encounter.

4. *Remember:* Fifteen-second resistance will show me the doors of escape from any temptation.

   a. The difficulty isn't the temptation: The downfall is in the hesitation.

   b. Don't worry with magnetism: Resist mulling the matters over.

SIX————

The Fifteen-Second Turning Point

"Our world traveler has returned," the postman called out to his wife when he opened their front door. "Welcome back. What did you discover?"

"I certainly have had an important adventure since I saw you last," Hope answered.

"Come in, and tell us what's happened." He held the door open wide for her.

"Welcome." Sterling's wife, Joy, hugged the sincere young woman. "We didn't meet earlier, but Sterling told me all about you. I know you've learned a great deal."

"I've written it all down." Hope pulled out her note pad and pencil. "I'm ready for you to teach me some more."

Joy offered her a chair. "What an eager pupil you are."

"I met with Dr. Cliff Climber, Carol Singer, Mercy Carrier, and Dusty Rhoades. They were all just great!"

"I think so," Sterling beamed. "Sure been good students, and what a difference they make in the world."

"They all know the fifteen-second secret," Joy added.

"That's obvious," Hope agreed. "You can't miss the happiness they exude. You don't find that often these days."

The postman leaned back in his chair. "Most priceless commodity in the world. If we could bottle and sell it, we'd all be millionaires."

"But I believe there is a basic ingredient," the sincere young woman continued, "that all of you people have and I don't. I sense that I need to know something else that is even more basic than what you have told me so far. I just don't know how to put my finger on what I lack."

"Oh?" Joy answered, furrowing her brow. "Try to tell us what you feel is missing."

Hope fidgeted in her chair. "It's difficult to put into words, but it came to mind when the coach talked about the total teacher. For example, I can practice fifteen-second convictions and practices, but how do I know the petitions really will work? How do I know that faith is stronger than fear?"

"Now I understand what you're asking us," said Sterling Veteran. "You have missed an important turn in the road. Perhaps this is the time to talk about the fifteen-second turning point."

"Turning point?"

"Yes," Joy added, "I think that you did miss a very important component. Sterling can tell you all about finding turning points."

"You've heard a lot from me," Sterling said. He rubbed his chin. "Actually Joy has her own story about discovering her turning point. Why don't we start with you, Dear?"

"If you insist," Joy agreed. "Have you ever had a problem with fear?" she asked the sincere young woman.

"Heavens, yes!" Hope nearly exploded. "I know that I began all of my frantic searchings because of a childhood experience I haven't been able to get out of my mind. I've spent thousands of dollars trying to learn how to stuff my fear back into the box."

"Hard to do," Joy said sympathetically.

"Nearly impossible!" Hope sounded frustrated.

"Serenity just isn't possible," Joy continued, "unless we find something or someone bigger than our fears. Our faith has to be grounded in a larger reality if we're going to find peace."

"Yes," Sterling added, "serenity begins in a personal certainty about your source of security. Joy, tell us how you came to your place of discovery."

"I'm sure that Carol Singer told you about the death of our son. We have shared similar tragedies."

"Yes, she told me."

"Before our son was killed, we were typical religious people. I certainly believed in God and tried to be a very moral person."

"We went to church occasionally," Sterling chimed in, "and followed all the holidays that religious people observe."

"I just hadn't thought much about what I believed," Joy continued, "until we received that terrible telegram from the army. After that day, my world was turned upside down and inside out."

"We had such great hopes for our son," the postman sighed, "and I guess we both placed most of our dreams and hopes in him."

"One morning . . ." Joy paused for a few moments, "all of my confusion came to a head. I realized that I had no idea what I really did believe about God. I wasn't angry with him as much as totally confused. I knew that God was there somewhere, but everything else was blurred and formless."

"Yes." The seeker nodded her head. "I really do understand. When I was talking with Dusty Rhoades, I began to realize that my perceptions of God were not the same as you have described. I don't think it's enough to have faith in faith. There's got to be more substance."

"Exactly." Joy picked up a book from the coffee table. "That insight was where my turning point began. I knew that my idea of God was like a picture frame hung around the universe. I needed a picture in the frame if I was going to be able to overcome my fears."

"We didn't get hung up in a 'hate God' problem," Sterling added. "We knew that wars and terrible accidents happen because people are irresponsible. I suppose that made matters easier for both Joy and me."

"Yes," Joy agreed. "I wasn't disillusioned as much as I was uninformed; that's where Jesus came in. Sterling was the one who helped me figure it all out. Tell her what you told me, Dear."

"I suppose there isn't anyone who doesn't believe that Jesus was a profound teacher," Sterling began. "At least, the most skeptical college professors agree on his importance as a teacher. But after our son's death, that idea did not grow. I started reading the Bible in search of peace of mind. Slowly but surely I began to see Jesus was the full embodiment of all that he taught. What he did exceeded even what he said. As I recognized how the man was greater than his teachings, I sat and started thinking of him as the total teacher."

"You're saying that we mustn't limit Jesus to being only a teacher?"

"Exactly. Philosophers, scientists, teachers, lecturers are all communicators. They get their ideas out through their words. But Jesus was truly unique because he didn't speak as much as he was the speech. He was a walking message. What counted the most was not that he had new thoughts about God but that he actually embodied God. Understand?"

"I'm not sure that I do." The young woman was puzzled.

"Joy often talked about her problem of the empty picture frame around the universe. I began to discover that Jesus was the picture we needed to frame."

"Oh," the seeker said slowly, "I think I'm beginning to see."

"Our faith isn't in faith," Joy joined in, "but our faith is in Jesus. When I turned that corner, I knew I had found the key to trusting someone larger than my fears. At that point I became a fifteen-second Christian."

"But he lived two thousand years ago," Hope protested.

"True," Sterling nodded. "But through the centuries Jesus has remained our contemporary because of three basic facts. He was the fullness of God with us. Moreover, he died for our sins. And his resurrection from the dead was without historical precedent."

"That's a lot for me to digest," the seeker protested.

"Take them one at a time," Sterling continued. "Because Jesus was the embodiment of divinity, he is timeless. He is at home in any century. When you get a good look at him, then you have seen God. You can really know what it means to trust the heavenly Father."

Hope nodded her head. "If Jesus is just like me, then it certainly does make it easier to understand God. Just the idea helps me grasp much of what I didn't understand before. But talk about sin has always been confusing to me."

"I think of sin as simply coming short of what God intended for me to be. We don't have to get caught in terrible or disreputable behavior." Sterling pointed to an Indian bow and arrow that was hung over the fireplace as a decoration. "Think of sin as shooting an arrow but missing the target. Sin is missing the bull's-eye that God set for us."

"Now that really makes sense," Hope said. "I haven't done much that anyone could write a book about, but I've sure failed to hit the best goals that I could have set for my life."

"Ah," Sterling continued, "and that discovery leads us to the best point of all. Jesus' death was for this issue. He died to restore the dignity that we lost because of our many failures. Moreover, he reinstates our lost position before God. When he died for sin, he canceled yesterday's failures and reinstated tomorrow's possibilities."

"Of course." Joy was very serious. "The resurrection of Jesus from the dead was very important to Sterling and me. Jesus' story is one of the ultimate victory of life over mortality. Because the bondage of death couldn't hold him, he is able to defeat the final source of all fear. My decision to trust him enabled me to be a part of what he had accomplished."

"When I saw that fact," Sterling added, "I knew we were in touch with the source of serenity regardless of what happened around us."

"The answer is in what happens within you," Joy explained. "That's the key to everything. It only takes fifteen seconds. The total teacher is able to turn our confusion and bewilderment into confidence and new beginnings."

"Most people are aware," Sterling continued, "of the most important news ever delivered to this world, but they fail to recognize what it can mean for their own peace of mind. Let me read something to you out of the Bible."

Sterling flipped through his Bible to a worn place in the back. "I've shared this passage with so many people over the years that I've almost worn a hole in my Bible. Let me read it to you: 'This is the testimony: that God has given us eternal life, and this life is in His Son. He who has the Son has life! . . . These things I have written to you who believe in the name of the Son of God, that you may know that you have eternal life' (1 John 5:11–13). The promise is that we can truly know."

"I would think that a person would have to die," Hope said, "to know that he had really received eternal life."

"Unfortunately many people lack the assurance that this problem is taken care of. Eternal life doesn't start when we die but when we have Jesus in our lives. Jesus brings a higher quality of existence to everyone who belongs to him."

"This is what he taught?" Hope asked.

"Actually," Sterling continued, "his teaching was secondary to his role in delivering us from the fears that destroy us. He is truly bigger than anything we will ever have to face."

"I learned," Joy told her, "that I don't have to be afraid of bad news and that I can really trust God because Jesus has taught me who God is."

"His victory over death," Sterling tacked on, "has granted us certainty in life! We found that to be solid truth as we faced the death of our son."

"I know these insights are extremely important for your sense of serenity," the young seeker reflected aloud, "but I don't know how to get a hold on what you are saying for myself. How can your insight make the same difference for me that it has made for you?"

"You haven't yet come to your fifteen-second turning point," Joy told her. "Once I crossed that line, the rest followed."

"Fifteen-second turning point?"

"Exactly," Sterling verified. "A person doesn't have to have all the answers and understand everything there is to know about the total teacher to decide that he will become their guide to God and that their faith will be grounded in him. In fifteen seconds you say 'yes' to him, and the rest follows."

"How do I do that?" Hope asked.

"My turning point," Sterling continued, "was the result of a friend asking me to read a passage from the Bible. He challenged me to accept that moment as God's special timing in my life. I've memorized the verse because it was so important to me. Jesus said, 'Behold, I stand at the door and knock. If anyone hears My voice and opens the door, I will come in to him and dine with him, and he with Me' (Rev. 3:20). As I read, my friend asked me if I had ever actually asked Jesus to come into my life. He challenged me to make a faith decision.''

"To decide?"

"Yes," the postman nodded, "this is the point where the fifteen-second secret begins. We are responsible for our own lives, and God never violates that freedom he has given us. Only as we make this first decision are we really able to make the rest that are so profound in producing serenity."

"I suppose," Hope leaned back in her chair, "that I have intellectually accepted almost everything about the Christian faith. I always assumed that what the Bible said was true although I didn't really know much of what it said. Certainly I have never made any significant decisions about living by what it says."

"Most people aren't hostile to what Jesus taught," Sterling added, "but they've never considered that if his teaching is true, it must make a claim on their lives. Unfortunately they can't receive the benefits because they really haven't accepted the product."

"I see." Hope rubbed her chin. "It's like there's a line drawn out there, and I have to cross it."

"Yes. For example, I often have packages to deliver, but the people aren't home. In such cases I leave a slip saying they can pick up their delivery at the central post office. The package might contain very valuable merchandise, and it does belong to them. But if they don't come to pick it up, they'll never have their goods."

"How do I cross the line?"

"I'd suggest that you go home after our conversation and read Revelation 3:20, the passage I just told you about. Remember that before the world was even created, God had his plan in mind for you. Jesus Christ is the ultimate solution to any problem you might ever have. Knowing that, you simply ask him to come into your life by telling him that you hear his voice and want him to be a part of everything you are and do from that point onward. Think you can do that?"

"Well," Hope said slowly, "perhaps I can make that decision."

"Let me share another concept with you," Sterling added. "I'm sure you've heard of repentance. Sometimes the idea sounds very old-fashioned as if someone were putting a guilt trip on us. But really the idea clarifies the decision you need to make. Fundamentally you are deciding to change your direction in life. Instead of doing everything your way, you decide that from here on out, you'll live God's way. You choose to do his will instead of your will. That's the heart of your decision."

"Oh, you've really helped a lot!"

"Remember," Sterling said, turning to another place in his Bible, "when we read these words—'knowing that you were not redeemed with corruptible things, like silver or gold, from your aimless conduct received by tradition from your fathers, but with the precious blood of Christ, as of a lamb without blemish and without spot. He indeed was foreordained before the foundation of the world, but was manifest in these last times for you' (1 Pet. 1:18–20). You see the connection?"

"Yes," Hope said slowly, "I can't be neutral about his death. The cross puts a claim on me, and I have to make up my mind about accepting his priority."

"Yes," Sterling replied. "There's no halfway business about something that is so very important."

"And his death," Joy continued, "is also a model for us to follow. He has given us a new life-style through his cross."

"So," Sterling smiled, "sooner or later we must make a decision. Like sand going through an hourglass we come to a moment when everything goes from one way of existing to another. There's a fork in the road, and we have to choose. But once we do, all the promises of God are ours. We'll know that we're on the right track."

"Can I be certain?" Hope asked.

"Sure." Sterling nodded. "Certainty comes not from proving this approach is true but by living out that to which you have committed your life. In fifteen seconds you can say 'yes' to a new way of life. Then as the days go by, you will see the evidence."

"While the decision is simple," the young woman said slowly, "the consequences aren't. Yes, you have brought me to a major turning point."

"And I want to suggest that you also talk with another of our friends," Joy added. "I know of few people who understand the significance of turning points as does Grace Goodheart. She is a lovely, cultured lady with a few surprises for you. I'll tell her to expect your call. She'll help fill in some of the blank spots."

"Oh, thank you." Hope stood up. "People with the fifteen-second secret are very exciting to meet. I'll look forward to visiting with Grace."

"Good!" Sterling extended his hand. "Now I would suggest that you go home and ponder your choices. The answer is in a person, not a proposition."

"Thank you both so much." Hope shook hands with each of them. "Once again you've really given me a great deal to consider." The young woman hurried out to her

car, but before she drove off she added another page of
notes to her journal.

The Fifteen-Second Turning Point: Summary

1. We must have faith in someone who is larger than our
   fears. We must have personal certainty in our source of
   serenity.

2. In order to trust God fully, we need to be able to see his
   face. Jesus has provided the picture that we need.

3. In fifteen seconds I can decide that these facts are true,
   and God will be my bulwark against fear.

4. I must have my own personal turning point.

5. *Remember:* My decision is based on the Scripture,
   which has proven to be true century after century.

SEVEN

Fifteen-Second Discoveries

Hope Moore watched the lights go off and on as the elevator shot up to the fifteenth floor. The hotel was unusually elegant with its plush carpeting and lush decor. "Grace Goodheart's doing all right these days," she said to herself as she walked down the hall looking for the right apartment. When she saw the number, she rang the bell.

"Yes," a dignified voice said through the intercom. "Can I help you?"

"Sterling Veteran sent me," Hope said slowly. "I'm Hope Moore."

Immediately the door swung open. "How glad I am to see you." Grace was a smartly dressed woman in her late sixties. She carried herself regally with a distinctive sense of style. "I'm so honored you could come."

"The honor is all mine." Hope shot a glance around the magnificently furnished apartment. The silk drapes blended into the rich tones of the wall covering. "What a wonderful place you have."

"Thank you." Grace Goodheart ushered her into the living room where tea service had been set up near the brocaded couch. "Won't you sit down and relax?"

"I suppose Sterling told you something about my quest?"

"Dear, dear man." Grace offered her a lace napkin. "He called and said you would be coming. What a marvelous difference he's made in my life. I'm sure that I will never be able to repay him for all that he has done for me. What a needy person I was."

"Needy?" Hope glanced around the room again. "I'm not sure that I understand."

"Beyond expression." Grace shook her head. "My life was in absolute shambles. Oh, but I was a mess."

Hope Moore studied the cultured face with the suave coiffure. Grace was something out of a fashion magazine or even a *Vogue* model. "You must be joking."

"Oh, no, my dear," Grace sighed sadly, "I never jest about the condition of my life before my fifteen-second turning point."

"That's what I'm here to talk about! The turning point."

"Without that moment in my life, I wouldn't have survived." Grace placed a little tea cake on a porcelain plate and handed it to Hope. "I'm sure I don't look the part, but you must understand that being an 'up and outer' is just as destructive as being a 'down and outer.'"

"Whatever do you mean?" Hope blinked. "I've never heard such a thing."

"Obviously Sterling didn't tell you much about my past." Grace faintly smiled. "He is so confidential, you know. But my life was in shreds when I talked to him the first time."

"Someone had died?"

"No, dear child," Grace Goodheart explained, settling back into her chair, "I had married and divorced three times, sinned lavishly, and lived a life of luxury that nearly cost me my soul. I was paying the high price of low living."

Hope stared, unable to respond.

"I don't look like it, but I am an alcoholic who only by the grace of God has this problem under control today. Surprised?"

"Well . . . er . . . a . . . I," Hope fumbled, "I . . . er . . ."

Grace made a sweeping gesture across the room with her hand. "Yes, my surroundings are a wonderful facade. With enough money, one can bury many things, but sooner or later, the hidden will emerge."

"Forgive me," Hope answered. "I just never associated such serious problems with affluence."

"Of course," Grace agreed, "our society portrays the rich and famous as the recipients of ease and well-being. The truth is that no amount of money or culture can compensate for the lack in our hearts, minds, and souls."

"Please tell me more of your story."

"I grew up in a family with great wealth. Most of my childhood was spent living in the Waldorf-Astoria Hotel in New York City. My parents sent me to the best girls' prep school and then abroad to study. I lived with nothing but the finest."

"What an exciting life."

"Yes, I had fairly well seen the world by the time I was twenty-four, but I hadn't read a Bible nor been in any church except the cathedrals I visited in Europe. My physical life was lavish, but my spiritual world was meager."

"You got into trouble?" Hope asked timidly.

"Oh, not for a long time." Grace shook her head. "I went through the years as if life were a continual fiesta of endless resources. But as marriage after marriage failed, the toll on my self-esteem and dreams escalated. Slowly but surely my drinking habits became apparent to everyone but me. Yes, I finally ended up in painful trouble."

"What happened?"

"I began to take pills. My doctors generally did what I ordered them to do. Eventually I took a pill to get me up, one to keep me up, and one to put me back down. Mixing the pills and the booze finally did the trick. When I woke up in the intensive care ward of the hospital, I learned what that concoction would accomplish."

"Oh, my goodness!"

"I didn't mind the suicide attempt as much as I minded botching the job." Grace offered Hope a cup of tea.

"But I thought—"

"No," Grace sighed, "I tried to put the best face on things, but the trip to the hospital was no accident. If my maid had not found me rather quickly, we wouldn't be here talking today."

"With so much money," Hope said, putting the cup down without drinking from it, "how could things have gotten so bad?"

"My life was filled with failure," Grace acknowledged. "My parents hadn't really cared enough to spend their time raising me. They sent me to school to keep me out of their hair. Each of my marriages was an abysmal failure. Most of my other relationships had been very destructive. I simply had lost all self-esteem. No amount of money can buy a reprieve from self-recriminations. I had nowhere to go but out. And that was when Sterling came into my life."

"Really?" Hope smiled, "I never cease to be amazed at the way he turns up."

"Postman makes all the rounds," Grace continued, "and he came to my house. I lived in another part of town then. Sterling showed up once a day. We spoke casually, but he was just another cog in my daily wheel until one afternoon when he brought a big package. I guess I looked like a frightful sight. I was about half looped and hadn't taken care of my appearance."

"Sterling said something to you?"

"Not at first." Grace ran her hand through her hair. "In fact, he was so accepting of me that I was disarmed. I had placed such heavy judgment on myself that I assumed everyone else did the same. Sterling didn't."

"He certainly meets people just where they are," Hope observed.

Grace shook her head. "Can you believe that I tripped and fell? So humiliating."

"Oh no!"

"He helped me up, and I started crying. But Sterling only said to me in such a kind way, 'You seem to be tired, Ms. Goodheart.' That was all he said, but he was so right. I was very, very tired."

"What an unusual thing to say."

"But he was so accepting. I found myself completely open to him because he met me at my point of need. I just wanted somebody to accept me as I was—in all my confusion. Because I felt so encompassed by Sterling's kindness, I was open to his guidance."

"How did he help?" Hope asked.

"First, he called for his wife, Joy to come over. Between the two of them and a pot of coffee, we made real progress. When my head cleared, Joy fixed my knee, and we began a friendship. They both observed that I seemed to be at a crossroads in my life. While I thought matters couldn't be worse, they assured me I could turn my confusion into something valuable. Their advice was the first encouragement I had heard in a long time."

"And that's how you came to your turning point?"

"I started there." Grace smiled. "Actually I listened to Sterling and Joy over a period of several weeks. I talked with some of their friends just as you have. As I look back, I realize that turning points are something like the constrictor in any hourglass. While the last grain falls through in just seconds, a lot of sand moves before that final moment arrives. But when I got to my decision, it only took me about fifteen seconds to cross the line."

"So a number of pieces in the puzzle had to fit before you could take the next step?"

"I'd put it this way. I'm sure Sterling has explained to you how our faith or fear determines how we make our difficult decisions. However, my dilemma came at a different point. Fear wasn't my central problem. Acceptance was. What I wanted most was to know that I was loved. Fear I could face. Rejection I couldn't. Serenity for me was a warm hug."

"So you were seeking love?"

"I didn't realize it at the time, but the failure of all the major relationships in my life had torn a huge hole in my soul. I felt extremely unworthy and without value. My sexual sins stripped me of dignity. Surely God couldn't be interested in me either. Then Sterling told me the story of another social outcast. Ever hear of Zacchaeus?"

"I'm sorry." Hope shrugged. "I really don't know much about the Bible."

"I sure didn't!" Grace reassured her. "But Sterling filled me in on many of the blank places. Zacchaeus was a very small man who was a tax collector. In his day, public officials worked for the Roman conquerors. They were collaborators, cheats, and extortionists. Obviously, the man was a real social reject."

"What happened to him?"

"When Jesus came to his town, all the people turned out for the visit. Because of the crowds and the fact that people scorned him, little Zacchaeus was forced to climb a tree to see the great man come by. Of course, the religious and righteous people were lined up expecting Jesus to stop and talk to them. As he walked by, Jesus looked up and spoke to only one man, Zacchaeus. He said, 'I'm going to your house today.' For Jesus to eat with this man commonly recognized as a social outcast was unheard of. In turn, Zacchaeus was given a renewed sense of the value and pride that had been stripped from him."

"I can see how that story really spoke to you." Hope sipped her tea.

"Somewhere between the tree and the ground," Grace continued, "this little man became a new person. In the time it took for him to slide to the ground, he began a new way of life. I suppose we might think of Zaccheus as being the first fifteen-second Christian."

Hope laughed. "Jesus not only was the total teacher but was the complete teacher. Hey, I like the sound of the phrase."

"Even though I had many great and varied opportunities, most people I know seemed to have a mean streak. People had been cruel and vicious when they were crossed. Many times when I was down, I was kicked. Thinking of Jesus wanting to go home with someone like me touched the deepest part of my soul. I wanted to be loved with such total acceptance."

"Oh, yes!" Hope nodded vigorously. "I think everyone yearns to be loved completely."

"Sterling told me that Zaccheus' story was a sort of parable about how the total teacher wanted to be a part of my life. As with the Judean outcast, he wanted to come to my house and honor me with his presence. Well, I just couldn't even imagine such a thing. What business would God's own Son have with someone whose life was as messed up as mine? I couldn't even fathom the idea!

"But Sterling kept after me. He had me read about Jesus being God's gift of love to needy people. With my own eyes I read Jesus' statement: 'Those who are well have no need of a physician, but those who are sick' (Matt. 9:12). Wow! Did that idea ever spin my head."

Hope turned to one side and looked out the window, saying, "I do understand. I, too, have lived so much of my life feeling unworthy. There are some experiences in my past that I avoid remembering if possible. I find it hard to believe that some of those mistakes could truly be forgiven."

"Honey," Grace answered, laying her hand gently on Hope's fingers, "there's good news today. Jesus really does come to stay with people like us. Sterling told me I only needed to ask him to enter my inner world and he would reside in my heart forever. He suggested that I ask God to give me the gift of faith to be able to believe it was true."

"The gift of faith?"

"Some of us have been so damaged by life that we can't imagine the scope of God's love and acceptance. We have lost the reference points that bring his acceptance into perspective. We need his help in even getting started seeing things correctly. We must pray and ask him to give us the faith to help our unbelief."

"And that's what you did?" Hope sat up in her chair.

"Yes," Grace said softly, "I prayed that he would help me be able to accept his acceptance. That simple prayer was my first turning point and only took a second. Shortly after, I finally began to see the meaning of Jesus' death on the cross as the final evidence of God's complete love for the world. Joy gave me a new word that did the trick."

"Joy has really helped me," Hope added. "She clearly understands God's love."

"Joy had invented a word to express her discoveries. She calls God's complete and total concern for us *omnicaring*.

"Ah!" Hope exclaimed. "That's the fourth word I'm supposed to learn. I've never heard of it before."

"Like the sound of it? I think the postman invented the word omnicaring. The more I used that word, the more I could see how Jesus' love covered every area of my life. Omnicaring meant that he could love others and me in the same moment. Omnicaring convinced me that his love would always extend into the future while being dependable even when others let me down. He will help me to meet today's needs and to face tomorrow's problems."

"I get goose bumps thinking about the possibility." Hope beamed. "Was omnicaring really valid?"

"One afternoon after Joy left, I sat down on this very couch and thought about my life. I honestly faced up to my drinking problem. It was out of control. I thought about the many lonely nights that were filled with pain. I remembered the many mistakes and sins of which I was ashamed. Then I recognized that omnicaring meant that I could honestly confess those indiscretions to him and face up to my need. He would truly love me, bad baggage, scars, and all. I got down on my knees right here in front of this couch. I asked him to take up permanent residence in this household. In those quiet moments my whole life pivoted. I found my eternal turning point."

"What a powerful story!" Hope's voice was serious and thoughtful. "I'm sure your life must have changed a great deal after that day."

"Oh, my," Grace said. "The changes were totally amazing. I found the strength to stand up to the drinking and the emptiness. I began to see myself with new eyes. I felt worthy and acceptable. No longer did I worry about what people had to say about my past."

"That change must have given you great freedom!"

"I recognized that many people had come after me with a stick. But God picked up those rods of accusation and punishment and turned them into a cross. He wrapped his love around me like a gentle blanket of kindness, and I was covered with grace. Can I tell you another little secret of mine?"

"Oh, do." Hope leaned forward.

"My legal name is Alice. After my turning point, I decided that I wanted to start anew in every way. Grace seemed like a more appropriate name. Since then almost no one calls me Alice. I like the new name for the new me."

"I don't know how I can ever thank you for the wonderful and personal insights you have shared with me." Hope opened her purse. "I keep a notebook of what I learn from talking with people about the fifteen-second secret. I've been so fascinated by what you've said that I haven't written a single word. I think I'd better get this on paper. I won't want to miss anything."

"Do come back and see me again," Grace said. "If I can ever be of help to you in any way, just call."

Hope placed her hand on Grace's shoulder. "I am deeply honored to know such a refined woman of obviously priceless value. You have made my life better."

Grace smiled. "Thank you," she said very quietly.

Hope hurried down the hall eager to write in her diary.

Fifteen-Second Discoveries: Summary

1. *Remember: omnicaring.*

2. The first step is to ask for the gift of faith so that I can accept God's acceptance.

3. Jesus came for the needy, imperfect, bungling people, for those who have seriously erred.

4. Jesus wants to be a permanent resident in my life.

5. *Remember:* Omnicaring means that his love covers both my past and future, what I know and don't know, the problems that I have now and the ones that I haven't yet faced.

EIGHT_____

Fifteen-Second Explorations

When the seeker returned to the postman's home, Joy met her at the door, and Hope realized that she felt like a part of the family. Now they shared a common experience.

"How's our newest daughter?" Joy hugged her. "Sterling and I hoped you wouldn't be gone too long."

"I crossed the line!" Hope blurted out. "I've made the decision, and now I know the heart of the fifteen-second secret."

"Wonderful!" Joy hugged her again. "Today you get a double welcome."

"You're marvelous! You make me feel as if I belong here."

"Of course," Joy beamed. "You do. You're truly part of our clan now. Come in and tell me everything that's happened to you. Sterling is on the phone. Can I fix you a cup of coffee?"

"I'd love one. I'll just sit with you in the kitchen."

"So you asked Jesus to come into your life and you've started on a new path?" Joy poured the steamy coffee into a mug.

"Sure did. I passed the fifteen-second turning point."

"Sterling will be so pleased." Joy handed her the cup. "Now everything you've heard will make much more sense and be easier to practice. And you'll be receiving that extra assistance Sterling talks about."

While Hope smelled the rich aroma of the coffee, she commented, "What started out as a search for serenity has turned into quite a life-changing experience."

"I'll tell you another little secret." Joy winked at her. "How could it be any other way? If we could have found peace of mind by living the old way, we wouldn't have needed to go on a new journey. No, most people will never know true, lasting fulfillment until they make very significant adjustments in what they recognize and practice as reality."

"Joy, that insight brings me to a question that I'd like to ask you while Sterling is busy. I have a friend who is in considerable trouble and I'd like to help, but I don't know what to do."

"What's the heart of the problem?"

"She's gotten herself involved with a married man and is in way over her head. The relationship has gone sour, and she's stuck with some things that she can't forgive herself for doing. She's eaten alive with guilt and doesn't believe there's any hope for her. She even thought about suicide. When she came to me for help, I didn't know what to say to her. What would you suggest?"

Joy looked out her kitchen window for several moments. Then she spoke: "I think that I would try to help her see that she is currently blocking her own capacities to experience fifteen-second serenity. She can't switch from fear to faith because her bad feelings have trapped her. She needs to practice one of the most important turning points of all."

"Another turning point?" Hope sipped her coffee.

"When we come to a decision that we want to avoid, we are at just such a crossroad."

"How do we confront this critical moment?"

"I have a promise from the total teacher that I refer to from time to time. In fact, a number of years ago I made a very serious error myself, and I used this help to get me past a necessary turning point in myself."

"I can't envision your ever doing anything wrong, Joy."

"Oh, yes," she sadly smiled. "I happened on a juicy bit of confidential information about an acquaintance who was rumored to be in the same fix as your friend. Before long I was sharing this load of trash all over town. The story was exciting and titillating. I guess I got a buzz out of passing it on."

"What's a little story?" Hope shrugged.

"Everything!" Joy said sadly. "I was guilty of murder because I was assassinating my friend's character. After it was too late, I found out my facts weren't correct and the story I was spreading was untrue. The people had to move out of town, and the results were horrible. I didn't think I could ever forgive myself. Even if my friend had done what I was passing on, my sin was far more damaging to more people."

"Gee." The sincere young woman flinched. "I never thought of spreading stories as being destructive."

"Any sense of serenity that I had was destroyed too. I don't know what I would have done if I hadn't found a promise based on what the total teacher brought us."

"Did Sterling teach you about this new turning point?"

"No." Joy shook her head. "Actually, Carol Singer was the source. I went to Carol to ask her forgiveness for telling the stories about this family. I was just horrified at what I had done. She was already ahead of me that time. Taking a piece of paper, she made a summary statement of my major problem. She wrote, 'Joy doesn't know how to forgive herself.' Then she quickly scribbled, 'I believe God.' Sound familiar?"

"Does it ever!"

"Next, Carol wrote out a very important line from the Bible: 'If we confess our sins, He is faithful and just to forgive us our sins and to cleanse us from all unrighteousness' (1 John 1:9). Carol told me that those lines applied to me and it was time to make a fifteen-second decision that they were true. I did."

"And that was the end of your problem?"

"No, it wasn't. In fact, I quickly discovered that I hadn't gotten beyond the crossroads at all. Several weeks later I saw the woman in a store. Apparently she had come back to town to finish their move. She walked over to me and told me how nice it was to see me. Her eyes were filled with hurt and pain. I could tell by her demeanor that she knew that I had helped to spread the stories. She seemed to be telling me indirectly that she had forgiven me. Yet the more that I realized what I had done to those poor people, the more the waves of shame rolled over me. Even though I was quite willing to make any form of restitution, I couldn't let myself off the hook. God had forgiven me, but I hadn't forgiven myself."

"What happened?"

"I decided to have another conversation with Carol. Obviously I was doing something wrong. Carol asked me the real turning point question: 'Why do you keep remembering what God has forgotten? The Book says, "Their sin I will remember no more"' (Jer. 31:34). That verse offered the turning point insight I needed."

"Tell me a little more," Hope asked. "I really have a hard time letting go of my mistakes."

"I think that most conscientious people do. But I discovered that if the verse is true, sooner or later God is truly going to cleanse me of all unrighteousness, even the pieces that I can't seem to release. I found that I just needed to stay with the process until the job was finished. My sins and mistakes were like a basket of apples. As I asked forgiveness, I removed the sins and mistakes one at a time. It took a while to get rid of everything in the basket, but eventually I did. We just can't give up on ourselves."

"What an insight!" Hope squeezed Joy's hand. "I've got a few apples left in my basket."

"Let me say it another way," Joy continued. "Recently I heard the story of a nun who seemed to have a remarkable ability to hear God speak. Her reputation as one to whom the Lord spoke directly soon spread. These reports fascinated her bishop. He decided that he would put her to the test to see if the rumors were true. Calling her into his office, the bishop asked, 'Is it true that God speaks directly to you and tells you what you ask of him?'

"The nun didn't want to appear immodest, but she felt she must tell the truth.

"'Yes,' she said, 'he answers the questions I ask him.'

"'Well, well,' the bishop said, smiling mischievously, 'I made my confession yesterday. Why don't you ask him if he can tell you what my sins were?'

"'I will pray and ask,' she said humbly.

"A week later the bishop happened to meet the nun during his visit to a church. 'Well, Sister,' he greeted her, 'did you ask God about my confession?'

"'Yes,' the nun answered. 'I prayed, and he spoke with me about your transgressions.'

"The bishop's face turned white. 'Good heavens!' he gasped. 'What did he say about my sins?'

"'He said that he had forgotten them,' the nun answered."

"I think you're telling me that there is no forgiveness unless there is also forgetting," Hope observed.

"Exactly. When I told Sterling about my experience, I was somewhat embarrassed to face up to the whole episode. However, he gave me a saying that he had read somewhere: 'Throw your sins into the ocean and put up a sign that says, *No Fishing.*'

"I had to realize that since God wasn't holding the error against me, I should not hold it against myself."

The sincere young woman started to speak, but Joy continued. "I've also learned that the serene life is not hard—it's impossible. I had to come to the realization that I couldn't live by myself. I had to have daily contact with Jesus to stay centered in his promises and the peace he offers. Otherwise, I would not be able to overcome my problems. That one insight was a major turning point."

Hope answered, "Your explanation is really helpful. Now I have something to tell my friend."

"Thanks," said Joy. "Two years ago, I wouldn't have been willing to say anything. I suppose we grow only as we live through the tough times."

"I guess you know that my husband and I have been in trouble. I don't have much hope for us."

"Yes," Joy acknowledged.

"Unfortunately, everything we try to do seems to end up in a disaster. We can't even talk without arguing. Prospects are bleak."

"You probably have a lot for which to forgive each other," Joy said thoughtfully. "The hurt must go deep."

"It's time for me to see if there is a turning point for our marriage," Hope sighed. "I think our conversation today has helped me see things in a new light. The change has to start with me. I've got to change my attitude before I can hope for any change in my home."

"Sounds like you're on the right track," Joy beamed. "You can't help but make progress if you're thinking along those lines."

"I've been blaming my husband for many matters that are really my problems. I keep letting resentments and old wounds fester. My lacking of forgiveness is poisoning the waters."

"Can you identify the source of these problems?" Joy pushed a sheet of paper in front of Hope. "Sometimes if we write these issues out and look at them, we can begin to sense what we need to do next."

"Yes, I know some of the problems, but mostly I've got

to put up a 'No Fishing' sign on my memories," Hope confided. "I have a bad habit of letting an irritation grow. I meditate on yesterday's errors the way a cow chews a cud. Since God has buried the past, I must too. I know *that's* the starting place."

Winking, Joy answered, "I have a hunch that once you've settled those old scores, it will be much easier to face the other problems that you and your husband have."

"I'm going home right now," Hope stood up resolutely, "and I'm going to settle these matters. Something wonderful can happen in my life because of the turning point I've found. There is new hope for our marriage."

"You'll certainly be in our prayers." Joy waved as Hope started her car and drove away.

Here's what the sincere young woman wrote later:

Fifteen-Second Explorations: Summary

1. *Remember:* Before I had the problem, God had the solution.

2. Don't keep remembering what God has forgotten.

3. I can't surprise God. He already knows the best answer.

4. Put up a "No Fishing" sign on your past.

5. Start by forgiving myself and my own past.

NINE _____

Fifteen-Second Directions

Hope paused as she entered the corner restaurant. She looked carefully around the room to see if Sterling and Joy had arrived.

Sterling waved from the table near the back of the restaurant. "Come on back," he called.

"We've been waiting for you," Joy said. "We got here unusually early because the traffic was lighter than we expected."

"I sure appreciate your taking time to meet me on a busy Saturday morning," Hope said. She sat down opposite her two friends. "I'm sure you have many things to do. But I really needed to talk with you."

"There's nothing more important," Joy replied, "than talking with you. We were glad for the opportunity."

"Absolutely," Sterling chimed in. "Tell us what you're thinking about these days."

"So much is going on that my head is swimming." Hope threw her hands up in the air. "I've been reexamining my decision to get a divorce. I never thought that would happen!"

"Well," Joy smiled, "our last conversation did make a difference."

"Big difference!" Hope exclaimed. "But I guess I can't decide whether it's good or bad. Looking at the foundations on which your life is built gets a little scary. I seem to be having second thoughts about what I'm doing."

"What we've told you is confusing?" Sterling asked.

"Oh, no," the sincere young woman said slowly. "Everything I've heard makes the greatest sense in the world. I suppose I'm afraid it won't work because the whole process sounds so easy."

"Faith is simple," Joy replied, "but it's not simplistic. You are dealing with profound answers."

"I keep a pocket Bible with me," Sterling said, pulling out a small black leather copy, "because all of our fifteen-second answers are based on this book which has stood the test of thousands of years. No one has ever proven it to be untrue. Long after the cities have disappeared, the Bible continues to be the all-time best-seller. You can know your decisions are true if they're based on the truths of this timeless book."

"Listen to the Psalms." Joy opened her own little Bible and read from Psalm 37:5. " 'Commit your way to the LORD; Trust also in Him, And He shall bring it to pass.' You can know your decision is real," she said, "when it is based on these promises."

"You're certainly reassuring." Hope took a sip from her glass of water. "I guess I just lack self-confidence."

"I certainly understand," Joy answered. "It's not been easy for me to live this new life-style. Everything was based on what I wanted to do. I've had to make a number of changes, too."

"But following the Bible is the answer," Sterling said, "because we know that we're following God's direction."

"Sure has been my experience," Joy added. "My sense of certainty grew as I came to realize the importance of knowing the Bible. The more I studied the Bible, the more confident I became in being able to understand what God has done for me."

"So," the young woman asked, "the Bible gives you the answers?"

"Yes," she said, "my knowledge of the Scripture gives me genuine balance. And it's helped me to listen to the pain of others and share God's conclusions with them."

Hope looked at the little book on the table. "How did you learn to use the Bible so effectively? It's such an ancient book and has always been somewhat of a mystery to me. You seem to use it in such a practical way."

"I suppose perspective is everything." Joy opened the Bible. "I expect God to speak to me through these pages. In fact, I think of this book as a unique receiver—a little like a radio. For example, we know that there are messages floating around this room on frequencies that we can't perceive. A radio tunes in these unseen messages. In a similar way the Bible opens up the channels to receive God's speech."

"But how do you tune in?"

"Basically I look for a specific application. I read with

an eye to a special word that fits my life. When I find what God is saying to me, the line sort of jumps out at me."

"Really?" Hope's eyes lit up. "How absolutely fascinating. God actually talks to you through his Book?"

"Yes." Joy put her finger under a line. "Here's an example. Recently I was very upset about a financial problem that we were having. I was really worried that we could quickly be in serious trouble. So I set aside time to just study the Bible carefully. As I was reading, I asked God to speak to me. My eyes were scanning the pages, but my mind was making fifteen-second petitions for insight. Suddenly these words seemed to come right off the page: 'Be anxious for nothing, but in everything by prayer and supplication, with thanksgiving, let your requests be made known to God; and the peace of God, which surpasses all understanding, will guard your hearts and minds through Christ Jesus' (Phil. 4:6–7)."

"Those words must have really encouraged you," Hope said, and she continued to read down the page. "I'm sure you felt a sense of relief."

"I knew that God was truly going to help us through the difficulties that we faced. And I truly knew that I was following the right approach. Even when circumstances are confused, this approach to the Bible gives me direction and a strong sense of self-confidence."

"So you read until some particular verse seems to have your name on it . . ." Hope wondered aloud, "and that becomes God's message for you?"

"There are many ways that people study the Bible. Some people look for scholarly insights into the past while others explore philosophical questions. All of these methods have a place and a value. But what people like you and me need is daily contact with his inspired Word to help us live with faith and not fear."

"That's certainly what I need," Hope agreed.

"Let me explain my approach another way." Joy picked up a pencil and a piece of paper. "You know that we're big on writing things down. When I find the verse that speaks to me, I write the entire passage on the top of the paper. Then I write out this question: 'What specific application does this verse have in my life?' I follow up by writing specific ways in which I'm affected or directed by the verse. I even write out the course of action I'm going to take on the basis of what I have read. By the time I've finished, I truly know how God is guiding me. As a result I'm able to maintain the daily connection with Jesus that keeps me centered in his promises."

"Basing your course of action on the Bible would have to give you reassurance," Hope responded. "I want to add this approach to the other ideas I've received so far. Great insight! When trouble comes along, in fifteen seconds you can call to mind exactly how God is directing your life."

Sterling said, "Our fifteen-second convictions all grow out of these biblical passages." He thumbed through the Bible. "I can't tell you that fact often enough. We haven't been giving you our opinions or conjectures. When you follow God's guidelines, you are standing on the most solid ground that will ever exist."

"I'm convinced that the two essentials in keeping our Christian experience alive are prayer and Bible study," Joy added. "That's one of the reasons why I'm so committed to the fifteen-second concept. The idea enables me to pray and read the Bible under any circumstance. Too many people are waiting for a special free time before they can work in study and prayer. They never find the opportunity."

"Your ideas," the young woman answered, "really are practical."

"Dr. Climber helped me discover the power of learning and using just one verse a day," Sterling continued. "Cliff helps people who have weight problems. He said reading the Bible before fifteen-second praying is like dieting."

"Boy, I need to hear this one," Hope laughed. "I just can't seem to remember not to overeat."

He grinned and patted his stomach. "Okay, let's think for a minute. What's the problem that most people have with dieting?"

"It's hard to stay on the plan?"

He agreed. "And why is that?"

She frowned for a moment and guessed, "Because we want to lose too much too soon?"

"Exactly! We want to lose five pounds a week or twenty pounds a month. And since the people who create diets know that's what we want, they say that's what their diets will do. But do they work?"

She shook her head. "No, not really. Maybe they'd work if we followed them; but evidently few can or we wouldn't always be looking for a new one."

"You're exactly right. Have you ever heard anyone advertise a diet program to lose half a pound a week?"

She laughed. "No, and I doubt if I ever will. That's hardly enough to bother with."

"Wait!" Sterling exclaimed. "Half a pound a week means two pounds a month, and two pounds a month is twenty-four pounds a year. Not bad!"

Hope thought for a moment. "Sounds different when you put it that way."

"You bet. And Dr. Climber says that according to the health experts who aren't trying to sell diets, weight lost at that rate has a better chance of staying off than the 'quick-fix' big losses. A little weight loss is not only more realistic, it will work better, last longer, and be better for the dieters."

"So reading the Bible is like dieting?" asked the young Christian.

"Exactly. The same principle holds for prayer and Scripture study. One verse of Scripture read and meditated on each day is 365 verses a year—and that's a lot of Scripture. The same is true with prayer; a one-minute prayer uttered several times a day, seven days a week, and fifty-two weeks a year creates a prayerful orientation toward life."

"The quality, not the quantity, is what matters, hmm?" The young woman blinked. "That makes a whole lot of sense and helps a lot."

"And," Sterling added, "like dieting you can't wait for the perfect day and the right circumstances. You take the fifteen seconds you have right now and get on with it."

"I think you're also telling me that successful people exercise the discipline of putting first things first."

"Good." Sterling leaned back in his chair once more.

"I guess," Hope went on, "I need to know a little more about how the fifteen-second convictions work."

"You remember those stories I told you about my grandfather?"

"Sure," Hope smiled. "I liked his down-to-earth approach."

"In the summer we would sit on the porch or rock in the old swing. Those were the times that he would tell me his stories. One day he laughed and patted me on the shoulder. Then he said something more serious than I had ever heard from him. He said, 'No matter what else happens in life, always remember these three things: believe, pray, and practice.' He had me repeat them over and over. And I acted like I understood them. Do you get what I'm aiming at?"

"Well," Hope said slowly, "I'm not sure."

"In a word," Sterling continued, "Grandfather knew that it's not what you say but what you do. People can say that they believe this or that—but what they live out is the key."

"And that is what you are trying to get me to see," Hope said thoughtfully. "I've got to practice what you're preaching. That's what makes the Bible passages really work for you?"

"Right! You can't just talk about it, you have to get into the action. My grandfather wanted me to understand that serenity begins with disciplined living. People are always flying off on tangents and running scared. All they need to do is sit still. In fifteen seconds they can practice remembering the direction that God wants them to take. That's where this fifteen-second business began."

"I think I'm discovering," Hope answered, "that I must recondition how I respond when difficulty comes along. My old way was just to react out of fear. But you are teaching me to respond to what the Bible says and not what I just happen to feel. Joy has been showing me how to let the Scriptures be the basis for those new reactions."

"Exactly! We focus our attention on the answer instead of the problem," said the postman. "You see, God's not sitting up in the sky somewhere thinking, 'I wonder what his or her problem is.' In fact, God already knows all the possibilities that can occur in our lives, even the seemingly insignificant ones."

"That's a rather big idea for Hope," Joy interjected. "I think you should explain a little more fully."

"Well . . ." Sterling began drumming his fingers again after pausing, reflecting on what to say. "Let's go consider my grandfather again. I know that he loved me and whatever he said was completely in my best interest."

"You're suggesting that God is something like your grandfather," Hope interrupted him. "He deals with us the way your grandfather treated you."

"Excellent!" Sterling snapped his fingers. "You've got it. But God is all-knowing and is all-powerful. Remember those words, omnipotent and omniscient?"

"Certainly." The seeker nodded her head. "You're teaching me that we can't bring him any surprises. He knows about everything and is in control of what seems chaotic to us."

Sterling thumped the table. "Excellent—but don't underestimate how much easier it is to say the words than to keep the principle. When our worlds are falling apart, we have a very difficult time feeling that God knows what's going on. Our prayers are filled with long descriptions of the gory details that we're sure will be news to him. We fret and fume because we're not sure he's fully in touch with our problems. It takes true discipline to act confidently on the basis of the omnipotence and omniscience of our heavenly Father."

"Dusty Rhoades gave me an example of this when he compared the process to doing karate exercises. I just have to practice until it becomes second nature."

"Definitely—and there's the punch line. Just like my grandfather, God consistently does acts of love for us."

"I have to admit," the seeker said, looking a little chagrined, "there are times when it does feel as if God has simply taken a vacation and I have been totally left to my own resources."

"We all have days like that," Joy acknowledged. "Sometimes the absence of God is the very way in which he is present to us. He appears to have left us alone because those times are part of his strategy to help us grow up. When we come to such a turning point, we have to make decisions that can be made only by ourselves."

"Those days can surely be very lonely," Hope acknowledged.

"When we are at such places, we have to remind ourselves that God is still all-powerful," Sterling reassured her. "Grandfather helped me to feel that truth before I could put the idea into words. As a boy, I saw a man for whom nothing was impossible. I believed he could make anything right. If my wagon was broken, he put it back together. So I grew up believing that Grandpa or someone out there was in control of the world."

"Sterling helped me comprehend," Joy told the young woman, "that God has a way of overruling even the worst of conditions and bringing something good out of disasters. I can count on his love to be at work in every situation I face."

The young woman nodded. "Carol Singer talked about fifteen-second convictions, which help us get in touch with God's concern for us when the fog and clouds seem to have swallowed us."

"Makes all the difference in the world," Sterling agreed. "I just remind myself that God is all-powerful, all-knowing, all-loving, and always present. No matter what the problem is, he already knows the issues inside out. In fact, God knows all the possibilities that can occur in our lives—even the seemingly insignificant ones. That's what I mean by believing, praying, and practicing."

"Sometimes when we have difficult decisions to make—" Joy hesitated, looking at the picture of their son "—we wish for someone we could talk with, someone who knows the answer. There is. It's God. He knows the answer that we're trying to find. Before the problem even comes up, God knows the best answer. People who practice fifteen-second convictions understand that truth and tune into God."

"I know this practice is easier to describe," the seeker thought aloud, "than it is to do."

"Somewhat," Sterling admitted. "There were many times that I found myself in a real jam. I couldn't see any way out. I'd run to God and cry out, 'You can't believe how big this mess is.' I would tell God about the size of the problem, mulling over again and again how impossible the conditions were. But then an image would come back to my mind. I'd see my grandfather down on his knees fixing my wagon. Before I even broke the wheel off, he knew everything there was to know about putting it back on. You see my point?"

"I'm getting the point," Hope nodded. "You just can't surprise God."

"Excellent," said Joy, patting Hope's shoulder. "God knows every possible answer, and most importantly he knows the best solution."

A light went on for the young woman. "These convictions help us identify our real problem and then relate it to the answer that God already has for us!"

"Very good," the mailman commended her. "Because we are studying the Bible daily, receiving the instruction that he has for us, we are already standing on a solid foundation. All we need to do is to take a fifteen-second pause to make sure that we're acting out of our faith and not from fear."

"Whew," the young woman sighed, "you've given me plenty to digest. Let's stop for now and start again later. I want to ask you some more questions about the power of God, but first I need to make sure I've really comprehended what you said today."

"Sure thing." Sterling looked at his calendar. "I'm going to be off work on Monday. Would you like to come over to the house in the afternoon?"

"Absolutely. I'll be there." Hope looked at Joy. "Before I leave, do you mind if I bring my notebook up to date?"

"We'd be glad for you to." Joy stood up. "Why don't you stay here at the table and write? We're on our way to another appointment. See you Monday."

Joy waved on her way out the door.

Immediately Hope began to write in her notebook.

Here's what the sincere young woman wrote:

Fifteen-Second Directions: Summary

1. Fifteen-second convictions are based on the Bible.

2. I need daily contact with God's Word. As I read, I need to write out specific applications for my life.

3. The Scripture will keep me balanced and aware of God's will for my life.

4. Rather than being fearful, I should identify the answer that God has already provided.

5. Serenity begins in disciplined living.

6. *Remember:* Believe, pray, practice.

TEN _____

Fifteen-Second Insights

Hope walked briskly up the walk to Sterling and Joy's house. Finding the door wide open, she called out, "Anybody home?"

"Yes, I've been expecting you," the mailman answered. "Come on in."

"Brought my note pad." Hope closed the door behind her. "I don't go any place these days without it."

"Excellent." Sterling ushered her into the living room. "Joy had to run to the store. She may not be back for our talk."

"I'm sorry I've missed her. But I have some questions for you."

"Where would you like to start?" Sterling sat down on the couch.

"I want to go back to the place where we left off last week." Hope took a comfortable chair facing the postman. "You were explaining the character of God."

"As I recall," Sterling said, "I was talking about how God is omniscient, omnipresent, omnipotent, and omnicaring."

"Tremendous words." Hope scanned her notebook. "Each concept has already had a profound effect on my thinking. I want to know more. How about expanding the idea of omnipotence?"

"Sure," Sterling agreed. "Very important. What we believe about God's power shapes our expectations of what he can do. Our faith will only be as strong as is our confidence in his sufficiency."

"Almost sounds like a math equation," Hope noted.

"Sorta is," the mailman agreed again. "You see, our problem is understanding how God's power operates. Unfortunately most people think of power as the ability to unleash force. We get mental pictures of a tank smashing over a hill or a tornado tearing a barn apart. In the mind's eye we see God as the ultimate strong man in a carnival. He can bend nails with his teeth and break chains with his hands. God's the final word in muscle development."

"Why not?" Hope shrugged her shoulders. "Making all those mountains and oceans took one huge burst of energy. Crashing of waves and the rumbling of thunder always make me think of God."

Sterling pursed his lips. "Of course, the big noises get our attention. Watching Niagara Falls certainly helps put us in perspective. But if that's all there is to God, we're only left with foam and wet spray. I find that the better symbol for his power is what happens downstream at the hydroelectric plant. Turning all of that force into constructive energy is a better picture of the power of God."

"Now that insight really fascinates me." Hope leaned back in her chair.

"I'm suggesting that creative power is the best way to think of omnipotence," Sterling continued. "God sees all that we can become and uses his power to help us realize our potential. What means the most to me is knowing that I'm just as important to him as the earth or the stars that shine across the Galaxy."

"My goodness," Hope gasped, "that's an overwhelming idea! You think we're that significant?"

"Sure do," Sterling answered. "That's where I got the idea of writing out fifteen-second convictions. God is interested in even the details of our lives, so we can trust God for specifics. Believing in generalities has a place, but if I'm going to conquer fear I have to know that God's resources are available to take care of my personal needs. That's why our convictions are based on Scripture."

Hope vigorously nodded her head. "The pieces are coming together. And you've given me something more dependable to hang on to than my feelings."

"Feelings fade, and fear disorients."

"I don't know about you," Sterling suggested, pointing at his chest, "but I know what my heart does when I'm afraid. The faster mine beats, the harder it is for me to think straight. At the most crucial times I need a source of certainty beyond myself if I'm going to remain stable."

"And the Bible provides the answers."

"Indeed," Sterling affirmed. "The Psalms tell us to hide his Word in our hearts. Feelings come and go, but memorization keeps the Book in place. Regardless of changing circumstances, I can hear God speaking when I depend on the answers that I find in those pages."

"But sometimes even when I know what the Bible says, I am still not sure what I should do. Lately I've been struggling with a situation that seems very confusing. I'm trying to follow the Bible, but I'm also not clear that I've taken the right path. What should I do when confusion shuts out the light of clear insight?"

Sterling leaned back in his chair and responded seriously. "After we have done everything that we possibly can and followed every direction that God has given us, sometimes there's nothing to do but love God."

"Why," the young woman said, pushing back from the table, "I thought you were giving me instructions that prevented uncertainty and indecision."

"Yes," Sterling agreed, "but life isn't a puzzle to be solved. It's a mystery that we live. At some time or other we will be faced with situations beyond our comprehension. At those moments we have no alternative but to trust and love God."

"*Just* to love God when I don't know what to do?" Hope puzzled.

Sterling thumbed through the Bible he took from the end table. He ran his finger down the page until he came to a particular line and started reading. "You shall love the LORD your God with all your heart, with all your soul, and with all your mind" (Matt. 22:37).

"And?" Hope gestured for him to continue. "Explain what those lines mean to you."

"Big part of the secret of serenity," Sterling chuckled. "When I continue to love God regardless of the circumstances, peace of mind grows and expands. I believe that my relationship with him is more significant than any particular solution. That's practical omnipotence!"

"Here's another angle," Hope said slowly. "I've come to see that Jesus demonstrated that same idea on the cross. I'm sure that none of his followers could understand what was going on when he was put to death. Yet Jesus kept right on trusting in the Father's love. While the rest of the world thought Jesus was no more, God was at work. Almost everyone in Jerusalem was sound asleep at the moment that he arose. His resurrection demonstrates what it means to keep on loving God during the dark times while waiting for the morning to come."

"Very good!" Sterling beamed. "That's a profound insight. In fact, I want you to tell me more of what you've been learning. I have a hunch you're loaded with great insights."

"I have been working at believing, praying, practicing. In fact, I've made a very important decision based on confidence in God's omnipotence. I have reconciled with my husband."

"Wonderful!" Sterling reached over and hugged Hope. "What an extraordinary decision you've made."

"I decided to trust in the power of God. Since God works through love, he surely wants to help my husband and me recover our love for each other."

"Joy will be so pleased. We've both prayed for your marriage many times. You've become walking proof of the power of God."

"I trust so. I suppose I'm counting on his omniscience as well. I believe that I can depend on him to know what I will never be able to comprehend. So I'm going to love God and my husband regardless of what I can or cannot understand."

"How important!" Sterling grinned. "Excellent application. Now tell me what you've learned about omnipresence."

"I read the story of Paul's shipwreck in the book of Acts. Remember?"

"Sure," Sterling answered.

"I was struck by how everyone on the boat was terrified except Paul. The sailors were in a complete panic while Paul was calmly praying that God would provide an answer. He was practicing faith in both God's omnipresence and omniscience. Paul knew that God was with him even though the circumstances seemed to deny the possibility."

"You *have* been reading your Bible," Sterling noted approvingly.

"When everyone fell screaming into the ocean, Paul was looking for how God was with him. Sure enough! Timbers from the boat were floating all around him. God was there. Paul grabbed one and began swimming for the shore. You might say that he found peace among the pieces."

"That's a superb example of omnipresence," Sterling responded. "God was there regardless of the circumstances. I find that people generally feel that God is with them only when things are going great. When the storms come, they think he has checked out."

"I guess we naturally think of God as being on the winner's side," Hope conceded.

"Certainly was true of Bill's thinking." Sterling rubbed his chin. "He worked with me at the post office. I don't think that I told you the story of what happened with his wife. We were good friends when their troubles started.

Jane got involved with another person, and the world came crashing in on both of them. I tried to help Bill understand the meaning of this really important verse: 'We know that all things work together for good to those who love God' (Rom. 8:28). But Bill couldn't see it."

"Same problem of feeling God's not on the loser's team."

Sterling nodded. "Exactly. All the marital strife settled over him like an ocean fog. Bill could believe God was there in quiet times of solitude, but during the chaos and confusion, he was sure God had abandoned him. Happens every time when people haven't figured out omnipresence."

"I'm learning," Hope commented, "that God's love doesn't change because the circumstances change. God is changeless."

"Yes. In the storm our anchor is hooked to the very center of the universe. The winds can blow and the world turn upside down, but omnipresence means that God's love remains."

"I have failed many times in my life." Hope's voice was low and intense. "And certainly I have failed in the past with my marriage. But I now know that God stands with the losers every bit as much as with the winners. The cross of Jesus Christ means that he loves people who fail and is with them in their desperation."

Sterling nodded and went on with his story. "Bill finally learned that was true. He began to recognize that God was working even if the problems weren't solved overnight. He decided to make the fifteen-second decision that he would live by faith and not fear. Once he crossed that line, he found stability in the midst of the chaos."

"What happened to his family?" the seeker asked.

"Eventually his wife recognized that she had serious problems and went for help. Her counseling sessions set the stage for them to work out their problems. As the relationship was mending, Bill found a great deal of fifteen-second serenity as he applied his convictions and kept sending up his petitions."

"Now let *me* tell *you* about omnicaring," Hope exclaimed. Her eyes sparkled. "I've been at work myself and have a story about one of my friends."

"Oh?" Sterling's eyes looked surprised.

"I've been sharing what you've taught me with a friend—Jack Hammer. Jack's one of those hard-driving, can't-take-no-for-an-answer salesmen. Lately he's been going through a crisis."

"I've met a few of those overwhelming types," Sterling acknowledged. "Sorta scare me."

"Actually Jack is a very sensitive, moral man. Yet he felt great pressure to make more money. He cut corners, cheated every now and then, and often took unfair advantage of people. Jack Hammer made lots of money by these questionable practices, but his methods weighed heavily on his conscience. Jack knew that he was going to have to make some changes to straighten out his life."

"Couldn't he just decide to be more honest?"

"He was afraid," Hope explained. "Jack grew up under difficult economic circumstances, and he was fearful of what might happen to him without financial security. Jack had a very hard emotional struggle to believe that God could provide for him. He needed help to face his fears."

"And you had the opportunity to explain omnicaring to him?"

"Yes, but first I helped Jack get in touch with the fact that in a quarter of a minute he could determine everything else that followed. He had to trust in both God's omnipotence and omnipresence. When Jack started practicing the fifteen-second principle, he began to see that God always works through love. Jack claimed the promise that at every moment God was working through his experience to make it turn out for the good. So he developed a new habit to take a first step. Before he made personal contacts or placed phone calls, Jack stopped and affirmed his love of God, his love for others, and his love for himself. Then he thanked God and told him that he would love him always. Only took about fifteen seconds."

"I'd like to do business with a man like that," Sterling noted.

"Of course," Hope smiled. "Everyone would. You can guess what followed. While Jack was only seeking serenity, he found that his business really prospered. Things did work out for him."

"Am I ever impressed," Sterling laughed. "You've arrived at the very heart of the secret. An often-overlooked ingredient in peace of mind is the art of forgetting about oneself. We do that best by looking out for the needs of others. You did that *with* Jack, and he in turn did the same *for* others."

"I can't just seek peace for myself," Hope acknowledged. "I have to help others reach the same goal. I believe that's how we know that we are for real. When my salesman friend quit taking advantage of people, he demonstrated that his faith was valid. People who aren't moved by the pains and problems of others aren't genuine. Turning points that truly connect us with God also bind us to others."

"Praying for others," Sterling added, "certainly helps us get started doing something for them. It's just practical omnicaring to care for others as God cares for us."

"Enough for today." Hope stood up. "Did *you* take notes this time?"

"No," Sterling laughed, "but I should have. You're doing fabulously."

"Thank you." Hope smiled. "I have certainly found my way into a new life. I did jot down some very helpful insights that came up in our conversation. Let's get together next week."

"I'll be looking forward to it." Sterling hugged her. "Maybe you'll have some more new lessons for me."

Here's what Hope wrote:

Fifteen-Second Insights: Summary

1. *Remember:* Omnipotence means that God's power is best demonstrated by his creativity. He will use his power to help me reach my potential.

2. *Remember:* Omnipresence means that I can always find peace among the pieces. He will help me rebuild my life.

3. *Remember:* Omniscience means that God already totally and completely knows what I can't and maybe never will understand. He will provide what I can't find for myself.

4. *Remember:* Omnicaring means that I care for others as I know God cares for me. I offer them the same wonderful love he gives me. Loving God, myself, and others makes my problems manageable. He will help me as I help others.

ELEVEN_____

Fifteen-Second Service

"Hello," the voice boomed from the receiver.

"Sterling? This is Hope."

"Yes. How nice of you to call."

"Catch you at a bad time?"

"No, no . . ." His voice was warm and pleasant. "Joy and I just finished supper. How are you?"

"Just fabulous. The last few weeks have been absolutely fascinating. My life will never be the same."

"Such reports are always music to my ears," Sterling answered.

"In fifteen seconds I found a completely new way of life. Who would have believed that so much could happen in such a short amount of time?"

"Around our place we call that a miracle."

"That's why I'm calling. How would you like to meet miracle number two?"

"Number two?"

"Yes, I'd like to drop by and introduce you to someone. Would that be convenient right now?"

"Sure. Joy and I will be waiting."

"See you in a few minutes."

○

The door was open when Hope and a man walked up the steps. "Anybody home?" she called.

"We're here," Joy's familiar voice called back. "Come on in."

"I have someone for you to meet, a little surprise for you," Hope said excitedly. The man opened the door for her.

"Hello." Sterling offered his hand. "I don't think I know you."

"Sterling and Joy, I want you to meet a very special person in my life. Meet Tyrone Moore, my husband. Ty, I want you to meet my special friends, Sterling and Joy."

"My pleasure." The tall, handsome man extended his hand. His black hair, penetrating eyes, and deeply tanned skin made Tyrone Moore a commanding figure. "I've heard so much about both of you. I owe you a great deal."

"Well," Sterling said, shaking Ty's hand vigorously, "this is a distinct honor."

"I feel like the honor is all mine." Tyrone Moore's rich voice filled the hall. "You've helped turn my life from disaster to promise. I am deeply indebted to both of you."

"What Ty's telling you," Joy beamed, "is that something very wonderful has happened. I wanted you to hear the story from him. I've been sharing with Ty everything that you've taught me over the last several weeks."

"Two nights ago it all came together for me," Ty grinned. "I fully realized what Hope had been telling me. I came to my own turning point and made that famous fifteen-second decision for myself."

"Ty became a Christian too!" Hope smiled happily.

"Good heavens," Sterling laughed, "now we have a spiritual son! Absolutely wonderful!"

"I call that real practicing." Joy hugged Hope. "Come in and tell us all about this turning point."

"I've not been hostile to religion," Ty began as he sat down on the couch, "but I have avoided contact with churches or religious people. Even though I would have said that I believed in God, practically I didn't."

"Tell us something of your background." Joy settled back in her chair.

"When I was about four years old, my mother and father broke up. I really don't know what the details were, but my father left us. I grew up without even knowing who he was. Times were rough, and mother blamed him for our financial woes."

"Sounds pretty bad." Sterling handed each person a cup of coffee. "I'm sure that time in your life left emotional scars."

"I'm afraid so. I guess I developed a deep distrust for the man who was responsible for my life. Without knowing it, my feelings slipped over into how I felt about God. Hope helped me face the fact that it was very difficult for me to trust God completely. Do you understand?"

"Sure do." Sterling set his cup down. "You'd be surprised how many people have a similar problem. They usually can't put their finger on why, but they aren't confident that God will take care of them."

"Well," Hope's voice dropped, "if your own father doesn't love you, it's hard to believe that God does."

"Yes," Sterling sighed, "I do understand how painful those memories are."

"During that period in my life, fear began to dominate my thinking," Tyrone continued. "Most of my decisions were shaped by an unexpressed but constant fear of the unpredictable and the unknown. While I didn't get in touch with the fact very often, my adult life was molded by the same nagging fears."

"And when I introduced Ty to the fifteen-second principle," Joy added, "I wanted him to know that he really did have an option. He didn't have to be controlled by this negative motivating force."

Ty squeezed Hope's hand and continued, "I understood instantly. I knew what it meant to make a decision between fear and faith. She touched a nerve deep, deep down inside my heart and mind. I knew that she had found the key to unlock the grip that fear had on my dreams and imagination."

Sterling folded his arms and leaned back. "I suppose sooner or later everyone has to decide between two fundamental orientations to reality. Life is centered and grounded in either fear or faith and love. That's the watershed issue. But the only place I know where we can find love at the center is in Jesus Christ."

"I've studied many strange ideas, philosophies, and groups," Hope commented, "but none even came close to suggesting such a promise."

"That one insight Hope gave me," Tyrone continued, "has helped me understand why I was always such a driven person. I was running from the fear buried at the center of my soul. No one was able to help me see that the basic issue in life was whether I could trust God or not. Then Hope gave me the fifteen-second principle."

"There are lots of strange ideas and interesting religious symbols around," Sterling acknowledged, "but the cross of Jesus Christ is truly unique. At that place our worst fears are turned into a final picture of love. All of us are afraid of death. Our fears begin in our concern for survival. But the death of Jesus on the cross demonstrated that on the other side of that final terror lies the love of God."

"What finally helped you put all the pieces in place?" Joy asked.

Ty pulled a carefully folded note from his shirt pocket. "I've got it written down on this piece of paper. Hope read this to me, and the words cut through the fog that had settled over my emotions. 'For God so loved the world,' Ty read slowly, 'that He gave His only begotten Son, that whoever believes in Him should not perish but have everlasting life. For God did not send His Son into the world to condemn the world, but that the world through Him might be saved' (John 3:16–17)."

"Well," Sterling said solemnly, "that sounds familiar."

"For the first time," Ty said, "I truly understood the death of Jesus. He is living and dying proof of both God's love and his total trustworthiness. I guess he looked beyond my facade and saw my true self."

"We are all debtors to grace," Sterling said seriously. "What more could I possibly tell you?"

"Ty and I really want to develop a different pattern of

life," Hope said earnestly. "We want to be new and competent people. I thought you might run through the fifteen-second process for both of us. Could you review some of the ideas for Ty?"

"Sure," Sterling drawled, "let me hit the highlights. The first step toward serenity begins when we decide to practice fifteen-second principles and procedures daily. The more we use them, the more effective and significant they become in our lives because we are creating new patterns. Once our responses are automatic, we just naturally follow the way of faith rather than fear."

"And that's what I'm trying to do." Hope opened her notebook. "I want my reactions as well as actions to be transformed. I was fascinated by Dusty Rhoades' example of practicing karate until it became second nature. At first some of my fifteen-second attempts felt a little contrived, but now they're becoming as familiar as an athletic maneuver. It's great to have habits that improve your life every day."

Sterling beamed. "Actually both of you are examples of one of the most important parts of the process. I shared with Hope, and Hope shared with Tyrone. I call that lamplighting. Our peace and joy grow and continue as we pass them on. I got the idea from the total teacher, who said, 'Let your light so shine before men, that they may see your good works and glorify your Father in heaven' (Matt. 5:16)."

"You're talking about what people like Carol Singer, Cliff Climber, and Dusty Rhoades did for me?" asked Hope.

"Sure. You came to them seeking illumination. They helped dispel the darkness by being lights. They gave you the spark to start your own inner fire—warming you with their concern and affection. Now it's your turn to pass it on."

"I can sure do my best," the young woman offered, "but I just don't have their sphere of influence."

"Remember," the mailman smiled, "the issue isn't sphere of influence but scope of awareness. We aren't able to predict how far the ripples of our actions will go. You have already done one of the most important things that anyone can do. You have been able to communicate the most important truth in the world with the person closest to you. Actually witnessing with our family members is the most difficult task of all, and you have done that extremely well. Right, Ty?"

"You bet!"

"Ty, you may not feel that you have a particularly large sphere of influence, but you really do. Look at me. All I do every day is just walk around leaving mail. But you've seen the results. All of the people you met found a new peaceful and purposeful life because I dropped by. If I can have that effect, anyone can."

"I suppose that our influence is really a matter of perspective," Hope acknowledged.

"And commitment," Joy chimed in. "Ty told us how John 3:16 spoke to him. Here's what 1 John 3:16 says." Joy opened the Bible on the end table. "'By this we know love, because He laid down His life for us. And we also ought to lay down our lives for the brethren.' Sometimes we're called to do something very dramatic, but most of the time we care for others by sharing the good news with them."

"That's exactly right," Sterling added. "Before I began delivering mail, I thought there was a special category of humanity out there who were the 'top drawer' people, the real shakers and movers. Then one day I noticed something that only a postman would see. Federal Express mail comes to everybody. We're all in the same category. Some folks get a little more press than others, but the real difference in life is made by the people who receive divine assistance. As a matter of fact, the world has been changed as much by people you've never heard of as by the headline grabbers."

"Really?" Hope asked pensively.

"Let me put it this way," Sterling continued. "Do you remember who taught math to Albert Einstein?"

Ty shook his head.

"Of course not." Sterling winked. "But without that person there would have been no theory of relativity. Got me?"

"Great insight," Ty acknowledged. "Some obscure person actually changed the whole course of history."

"Yes," Sterling continued. "Who taught Abraham Lincoln to practice law? No one knows, but without that source of inspiration, the slaves would have never been free. Such a host of unknowns is continuing proof that every one of us has far greater influence than we would have ever dreamed. We can start chain reactions that will literally go completely around the world."

"I never thought of my life as having such potential," the sincere young woman replied. "But during the last several weeks, I have seen the difference I can make."

"All of us who share the fifteen-second secret do!" Joy exclaimed. "We seize the moment at hand and can make a permanent difference in someone's life. And how did you feel when you saw the results your sharing brought to Tyrone's life?"

"Inexpressibly wonderful! I've been through plenty of self-hype trips, but this feeling was different. I knew that the love of God was being conveyed through me. Nothing compares with that awareness."

"Only took about fifteen seconds," Sterling chuckled again, "and the results will last for eternity. The principle always works. We can keep only what we give away. Something of what you lost from the bumps and bruises of life came back to you because of what you gave to him."

"Oh, my goodness—" Hope put her hands to her mouth. "I don't know what to say." Tears filled her eyes. "I'm overwhelmed. I had no idea that I was getting into something so deep."

"All those New Wave gimmicks you pursued," Sterling said, patting her hand, "were only Band-Aid attempts to cover a huge hole in your soul. Now you're dealing with the stuff of true healing and wholeness. Did you ever hear of Augustine?"

"Wasn't he a famous ancient philosopher?"

"Yes," Sterling confirmed, "he was a fourth-century Christian leader who recognized that we have an inner God-shaped vacuum that nothing but God can fill. His famous conclusion was, 'We are restless until we find rest in Him.'"

"I'm amazed to realize that something so profound and powerful has happened to us in such a short time." Hope kept shaking her head.

"As we help others," Sterling answered, "we are able to find the help that we need. I want you to keep on doing what you have begun with Ty. Peace of mind comes as we help others find their own source of serenity."

"I have never done anything as gratifying as helping my husband. I've been on lots of committees and sponsored many projects, but seeing him leave fear and self-recrimination behind was totally fulfilling."

"You were applying that basic principle," Sterling instructed. "You can keep only what you give away, and that is how you can repay me. Just pass the fifteen-second secret on to others. We'll all reap serenity in new measure, and the world will be a much better place."

"I never realized what a difference I could make," the sincere young woman reflected. "Every person I meet is a candidate for my message."

"It only takes fifteen seconds," Sterling noted. "We don't worry about long speeches or dramatic presentations. In a few moments share the fact that in a world of turmoil you have found the path to well-being."

"I know that there are people around me with overwhelming needs for what I've learned." Tyrone sighed deeply.

"A popular expression of fifteen-second sharing is 'one beggar telling another where bread can be found,'" Sterling said. He added, "Our problem is that we think of beggars as being crippled indigents in rags. Actually, we are surrounded by men in $500 business suits and women dripping with diamonds whose inner worlds are more poverty-stricken than those of the masses on the streets of India. We must see behind the facade and recognize that our poor rich people are as void of serenity as the Sahara is of drinking fountains."

"I know that I've often walked around with my eyes wide open while my heart was completely closed," Ty admitted. "But both of you have started me on a new journey."

"I think of us as being in the mail business," Sterling smiled. "We have been charged with making sure that God's special delivery letters get through. We don't have to be big, brilliant, or beautiful. We simply need to be alert to human need."

"I think that I could spend the rest of my life doing what you just described," Hope replied. "I'd be happy being part of helping others find fulfillment."

"That's really the final step in the fifteen-second secret," Sterling concluded. "We have all been commissioned to pass the message on to others. Fifteen-second Christians are like the post office; nothing keeps them from getting the message delivered."

"I'm ready," Tyrone declared. "Ty Moore will be Try Moore from now on."

Hope reached over and put her hand on the mailman's arm. Looking him straight in the eye, she said, "You've made a complete difference in my life. Now I'm going to do the same for a multitude of others. Thank you for caring about us."

Sterling and Joy watched the young couple walk down the driveway and get into their car. The older couple felt grateful and serene knowing that they had been able to bring warmth and light to a cold and dark world.

Later in the day, Hope Moore sat quietly by her bedroom window looking out over the garden where her husband was happily working. She wept as she realized how close she had come to losing her family and home. Now they were a unit happily tied to the same eternal center.

Hope thought of her friend the mailman walking down the street, always about the business of making the world a better place. She felt proud to be on the same team.

Some new person would look up from a desk and see this confident happy man and ask about his secret. In fifteen seconds, he would begin to make a permanent difference in that person's life.

"But maybe—oh . . ." For a moment she felt apprehensive. "I don't know if I can really stand up to such responsibility. . . . Wait a minute," she continued to reflect aloud. "What am I saying? Fear has no place in my vocabulary. The journey of a thousand miles begins with the first step. I can be available for whatever needs to be done. I'm just as much a fifteen-second Christian as the others."

With that, Hope Moore started housecleaning again. She hummed as she busily finished up her tasks. Suddenly she stopped and looked in the mirror above the couch. For the first time in her life, she was completely serene.

The last entry the young woman made in her notebook was:

Fifteen-Second Service: Summary

1. *Remember:* The more love I offer to others, the more I get back.

2. We can keep only what we give away.

3. I am called to be a lamplighter.

4. The issue is never sphere of influence, but scope of awareness.

5. I am of greatest value where I am right now.

6. *Remember:* The cross of Christ is the guarantee of God's trustworthiness.

PASS IT ON!

About the Author

Larry Jones is president of "Feed the Children" and director of Larry Jones International Ministries based in Oklahoma City. He received bachelor's degrees from Oklahoma City University, in arts and science, and from Phillips University, in divinity. He also studied at Moody Bible Institute and Southwestern Baptist Theological Seminary.

In addition to *Practice to Win*, which sold more than 200,000 copies, Jones has written *Build a Brand New You, Feed the Children, How to Bend without Breaking*, and *How to Make It to Friday*.

He lives in Oklahoma City with his wife of twenty-nine years, Frances.

If you'd like to correspond with the author of *The Fifteen-Second Secret*, please write:

Larry Jones
P.O. Box 36
Oklahoma City, OK 73101